to Jane Comporere with
best wishes and deep
appreciation for all
you are doing for ADA

FINDERS

KEEPERS

To All Who Join Me In Finding And Keeping

To all the men and women I've met and worked with through the years, extraordinary professionals and volunteers, and to those yet to find their own passion and commitment to the world of philanthrophy—this book is a celebration. It is a wondrous and exhilarating journey we undertake. I feel blessed to be traveling the same road with you.—jp

A man who knows not how to write may think
this is no great feat, but only try to do it yourself
and you will learn how arduous is the writer's task.
It dims your eyes, makes your back ache and knits
your chest and belly together. It is a terrible ordeal
for the human body.

So, gentle reader, turn these pages carefully and
keep your fingers far from changing the text.

Friar Robert Alden
C 1300 AD

Library of Congress Cataloging-in-Publication Data
Panas, Jerold.
    Finders keepers : lessons I've learned about dynamic fundraising / Jerold Panas.
      p. cm.
    ISBN 1-56625-116-8 (hc.)
      1. Fund raising—United States—Handbooks, manuals, etc.
    I. Title.
    HV41.9.U5P35   1999
    658.15'224—dc21   99-19738
                                                     CIP

Printed in the United States of America

04 03 02 01 00 99   1 2 3 4 5 6

Bonus Books, Inc.
160 East Illinois Street
Chicago, IL 60611
www.bonus-books.com

Finders Keepers

PART I

GETTING THE GIFT

1
Finders Keepers—
Losers Weepers

"You mean that's all there is to it?"

I'm talking with Scott Ascen. He's chairman of the $100 million campaign for Groton School.

If elite means: choice, select, and the finest—that's a perfect description of Groton. It is the alma mater to some of the nation's top corporate leaders, financiers, and high-ranking government officials. It lists among its graduates a United States President, a Secretary of State, Cabinet Members, and a host of Senators and Representatives.

Scott Ascen brings a riveting focus, persistence, and optimism to the chairman's post. All blended together in an unbeatable combination that is certain to ensure the campaign's success.

Back to our conversation.

He asks: "You mean that's all there is to it?"

"Well, there's a bit more to it than that," I say, "But that's just about the essence of it. You identify those who have the capacity to make the largest gifts. That's where it begins. You do whatever is appropriate to get the gift at the highest level possible. Then you establish an ongoing cultivation process that ends with the ultimate gift."

Scott says: "So that's what it's all about. You find your best prospects and you keep them. It's sort of like, *Finders Keepers.*"

Obviously, there is a great deal more to it than that. But it begins with identification, finding the prospect. The process then continues through a series of steps, best identified as the **6 Is**:

1   **Identify** . . . Begin by finding the prospect.

2   **Interest** . . . you find a way to capture them in your institution's net.

3   **Involve** . . . they participate in some of your programs, perhaps serve on a committee, attend an activity.

4   **Intervene** . . . you find a means to regularly *get in their way*, you intervene in their life.

5   **Invest** . . . you are ready to ask for the gift, they invest in your great cause.

6   **Influence** . . . most important step of all, you engage these enthusiastic investors to influence their friends and others to become interested and involved in your mission . . . the cycle continues . . .

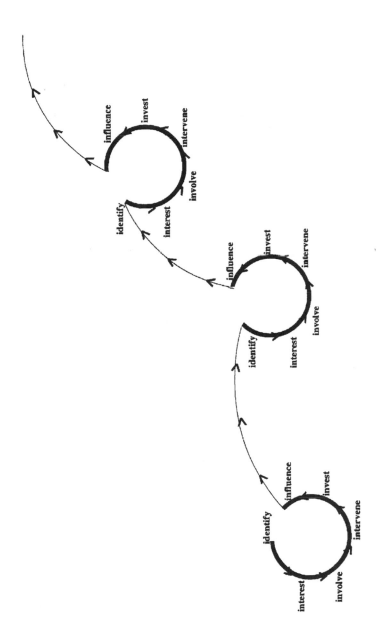

The Continuum of Is

Follow this cycle and it ensures you of finding and keeping your donor. It doesn't have to work in perfect order. As in ballet—which is the most beautiful way of moving the body between two points, but not the most direct, this cycle works at its most effective best when you don't miss any of the steps.

Go from identification to directly making the ask, and you run the risk of not getting the gift, or getting a much smaller gift had you touched each base. I am not without my own admiration for hocus-pocus, like the smoke-and-mirror tactics of Milo Minderbinder and *Catch-22*. He buys eggs at four cents each, sells them for three cents, and makes a penny profit. But in the kind of fundraising I'm going to describe, that doesn't work.

Your job is to get your people into what I refer to as the *fundraising hug*. You get your prospects interested and involved in the program. The more they get involved, the more they love you. And the more they love you, the more they give. Get your arms around them in *the fundraising hug* by going through each step of the cycle.

Asking for a gift is not about raising money. It's about nurturing. It's about winning people to your cause, developing leadership and ownership. It's about deepening commitment.

I love the life-changing way I can get into a person's soul and heart. I revel in the way I can engage them in a cause that is spirit-empowering and will have an impact on an institution for generations to come. For those moments, you have available the whole universe of a person's life. You hear it all. The pain and suffering, the exhilaration and the struggle. It is a never-ending joy to have your life intersect with theirs. You walk among the angels.

Finders Keepers is about integrity fundraising. That's because there is principle to the process. And faithfulness and completeness. Integrity, like finding and keeping the prospect, is not a destination—it is the road sign for your journey. Never compromising those things that are important to the donor makes a difference. It's what Thomas More referred to as *discovering the soul*.

In the kind of integrity fundraising I'm talking about, you're not raising money. You're helping people find meaning in their lives. They will never look back. They will want to go forward. To see more, do more, give more. They will forever be on a mission to help change lives and save lives. Dr. Morris Schwartz was a professor at Brandeis University. He said that once you learn how to give, you learn how to live. That says it all. With the people you call on, you make it happen.

Several months ago, I had just finished speaking to a large group at the Marriott in Kansas City. The speech was short of brilliant, but not bad. I had spoken about integrity fundraising and ensuring the gift. I finished and was in the elevator going back to my room. One of the attendees cornered me. The elevator is a difficult place to get away from someone.

He said: "I have been calling on this rich so-and-so for years, and I can't get a gift. Tell me what to do."

Thankfully, I got off the elevator before he did. Imagine giving advice to that kind of a question between floors!

I think I have the answer. There's an old legal axiom: *To delay is to deny.* That rich so-and-so very likely decided long ago that he wasn't going to give. Go on to a better prospect. with integrity fundraising, that almost certainly could not have happened. I'll explain.

You sometimes will receive a gift after you have labored unsuccessfully over a prospect for years and years. But it doesn't happen often. It is mostly laboring in the wilderness. Gifts and achievements in this sort of a situation can happen, but are rare indeed. As Peter Drucker says: "Most of the people who persist in the wilderness leave nothing behind but bleached bones."

Integrity fundraising is an art, constantly besieged and compromised by the researchers, technocrats, and giants of computers—the *science* people of our profession. They wildly miss the major focus of everything we do. The business of fundraising is after all, the nurturing of people. It is far more than *selling gifts.* It is a people business. An effective fundraiser empowers a person to do great things for towering causes. It accelerates the donor to levels never before anticipated, joy without parallel. Michelangelo said that *"a sculpture is imprisoned in a block of marble, and only a great sculpturer can set it free."* That's it, that's how I see the role of a fundraiser.

Your One-Two Punch

The job of the asker (staff or volunteer) is to create an understanding of the mission and vision of the institution. And then, secure the necessary funds in order to perpetuate that mission. One, two—that's how basic it is.

It is far more than money. It's spiritual. It has to do with human values. It has to do with dreams and unending aspirations.

Integrity fundraising is an exchange of values. It is not something you do to someone. It is something you do for and with someone. It means understanding the wants and needs of the men and women you call on. This is essential before you proceed with any attempt to ask for a gift. It means developing trust, faith, and rapport. You measure people by the depth of their heart, not by the size of their bank account.

Getting the gift isn't a victory for the fundraiser. It is a victory for the institution and most of all, for the donor. Everyone wins. It is a win-win, life-changing love affair.

Your prospect is a real person with concerns, needs, pain, and moments of joy that know no bounds. It is essential that you understand the needs and wants of those you are calling on before you ask for the gift. To do otherwise is to attempt to leap a chasm in two jumps.

You must develop a trust and rapport before any asking begins. This will take a number of visits. I know you didn't want to hear that, but in integrity fundraising in order to get a gift at the proper level, you can't kiss a prospect on the first date.

You *listen the gift*. More about that later. It's important that you spend enough time with the person and listen carefully so that you know precisely the amount you should ask for and the level of interest for a particular project. You'll know this by listening. If you haven't yet determined the prospect's enthusiasm for the project or the amount you should ask for—you are not ready to ask for the gift.

In integrity fundraising, finders keepers, crafty selling techniques give way to donor-empowering precepts. Hotsy-totsy selling methods (getting them to say *yes* to a series of questions before asking for the gift) are superseded by principles and high standards. Relationships built on integrity assure successful asking, and leave donors with a high level of satisfaction and achievement. This is no place for the *99 tricky closes*. The old strategy to out-talk, out-maneuver, out-think prospects is exactly why the elevator conversation I reported earlier was unthinkably naive.

Don't Fake It

You should develop a high regard, even an affection, if possible, for the donor. If that type of relationship does not exist—it shows. It really does. Don't fake it! Pass the prospect on to a colleague, another volunteer, or a staff person.

The fundraiser's high level of integrity will contribute more to the success of achieving the gift than techniques. The old rules of *close fast, close early, close often*—are simply rubbish. It doesn't work in integrity fundraising.

Pressure is never exerted by the fundraiser. If there is any pressure, and there should be—the pressure needs to be fired within the prospect. They sense the urgency. They understand how their gift can save lives or change lives. They feel the satisfaction of the gift. They anticipate the joy. The pressure is building—the prospect wants and needs to make a gift. It will happen. I promise.

To enable the donor to make the gift that he or she really wants to give, some careful probing will be necessary. In *listening the gift*, the emphasis is on inquiry and examination. You listen. A *no* does not always mean a *no*. It very often means: *Not just yet.*

Motivating your prospect is the totality of tremendous trifles. You anticipate, adopt, act. But it takes time. It's what Lyndon Baines Johnson said about politics: "It isn't hard. All you have to do is hang around long enough."

You can be certain you'll achieve your objectives. It will require some sort of a management system that enables you to monitor your top prospects—the contacts you make, their status, and their readiness to make a gift at the highest level possible, and finally an ultimate gift. The system is widely known in our field as *Moves Management.*© The name is registered and protected by the Institute for Charitable Giving.

Moves Management©

In *Moves Management*, or in any effective prospect and donor management system, call it any name you wish—you bring your donor closer to a *yes*, you achieve predetermined cultivation goals, you are able to measure the success of the contact, and there is a built-in follow-up.

The system is fail-safe. You can't miss. You don't, by the way *manage* the prospects and donors. The system manages *you*—to be more effective. The more I work in the field, the more I realize the critical importance of not violating the cardinal principle of asking the donor for a gift before he or she is ready. *Moves* guarantees that won't happen.

It probably means a number of contacts. You make the calls in a way that doesn't seem contrived, even though they are scheduled. Each call builds on the next. Never lose sight that your ultimate objective is not to make calls—but to raise funds.

In integrity fundraising, you will secure 10 to 25 times what the person has given annually. It will be a large enough amount that the person has to take time to think about the gift. My friend, Bill Sturtevant, calls it a *stop-and-think* gift. If it turns out to be a quick decision, you likely haven't asked for an amount at a high enough level.

It is a visceral decision. Emotions run fast and high.

In virtually all cases I know of, a spouse is involved in helping make the decision. As a matter of fact, my definition of a major gift is one *where the spouse is involved*. If the spouse doesn't participate, chances are it is not a major gift.

Make certain you never waste anyone's time. Don't have a meeting unless you have something that the prospect is going to perceive as being valuable. This is not a social call.

Your mission is to understand the needs of the prospects. Not to tell your story—but to listen to the prospect. You probe. That's not very creative or complicated—but it does make it quite clear. The early meetings are to better understand the person you hope will join you in your great cause.

The contact has to generate the kind of information and chemistry that provides for a good follow-up letter and an additional call. If it doesn't, you probably shouldn't have had the meeting.

Don't Start by Selling

And what is most important in integrity fundraising is that in these sessions, you don't start by selling. You start by understanding the prospect and listening.

Don't start talking about the gift unless you are absolutely certain about the needs of the donor and his or her motivation.

Try doing this. It takes time. I'm impatient and I don't like going through the steps (can you identify with this?). But it is worth it, I promise.

I use 4x6 cards. You can do it on a Call Report sheet or on your computer, if you wish. I like 4x6 cards. I can shuffle them, stack them, and rearrange them. They work for me. Use whatever works for you. Indicate the prospect's most prevailing wants and dominant needs. Put it in writing. Indicate how this program might meet those needs.

There's something magical when you put it in writing. It indelibly identifies what this investment is all about.

When you see the prospect again, don't talk about dollars. That's not really important. Talk about the prospects' needs and wishes. Keep probing. Keep asking for their opinion and how they feel about the program.

There are some questions that you need to get around to. Examine what kind of human or social return they want on the gift-investment they will be making. Ask questions that will be open and call for specific answers. Keep asking for their opinions and evaluation. And finally, ask what kind of outcomes they hope to achieve.

Only now are you ready to talk about amounts.

It has taken me a long time to learn this, but I am finally convinced: Donors give when they are ready to, not a moment sooner. No matter how urgent your request and the needs—the donor rules. By pushing too hard, the fundraiser can actually slow the process.

It is essential that your prospects understand the benefits they will enjoy from making the gift. And how their gift will help save lives and change lives. It's important to talk about the well of satisfaction they will feel. All donors feel the joy of making a gift. As one donor told me, *it was like the top of my head was spinning off.*

It somehow all works together, "the experience of the eternal truths and verities," as William Faulkner puts it. Fundraising isn't about raising money. It is a seamless fusion of magic and principles, benefits and details, art and science. There is a clarity of light that author Virginia Woolf saw as *moments of being*, those privileged times when truth is perceived in a flash of intuition.

I have heard that next to getting shot at and missed . . . there is nothing quite as exhilarating as getting a gift at the right level. You're on your way.

Fundraising is about building relationships and helping those with resources know where to invest their funds. Fundraising has to do with helping potential investors know everything there is to know about your institution. Having them know how you provide a service that is uniquely your own—and how their gift alone, will make a difference.

It isn't easy. Have you noticed how much harder you're working, how much faster the track is, how much higher the hurdles? The competition is getting keener for the philanthrophic dollar. Other institutions are calling on your prospects. And there is less time to tell your story.

Getting a person's attention today is exceedingly more difficult. People have more options to choose from, and many of the institutions look like you and sound like you.

There are more places for donors to give their money. If missions become blurred and fragmented, the institution is in trouble. The great lesson today is that no one any longer *owns* the donor. Losers Weepers!

More and more, I find that we have to take a much better look at our donors. We need to be driven by their needs and wants. And yes, at times, their demands. We need to learn about them inside-out. Get inside their heads. Become passionate about them.

There are more and more institutions competing for the people you hoped *belonged* to you. A never ending array of institutions are clamoring for their attention. It will be increasingly difficult to make them aware of you.

Your donors are better educated, more discriminating, far better informed, and have a different value system. They are iconoclastic and less loyal. Commitment is not easily won. Once you have it, you have to continue working in order to keep it. (Losers Weepers.) The race gets faster, the track gets slicker.

Old Loyalties Don't Count

Here's what I am finding. There's a lesson here for you. You have to fight for your share of the donor-market. It's from a smaller pool that you will have to get the gift. Old loyalties don't count. You have to win your donor all over again. Every day.

There is no longer the security of having a great and honored institutional name. Particularly with tomorrow's donors. They have little memory for old, *trusted brand names*. The biggest mistake is saying that you will keep up with tomorrow's donors because you have in the past. That will doom you to think that tomorrow will be just like today, only in a different place—just like Philadelphia, only with good restaurants.

Finders Keepers, Losers Weepers. That pretty much says it all. To identify your donors and keep them bonded to your institution, unalterably welded to your mission and cause.

Your job is to involve people in programs of towering proportions . . . to make true believers from those who do not know the full story of your work . . . to make joyful investors out of those who in the past may have only been contributors.

No easy task, this. But I shall prescribe a process that I am convinced will help you win your gift. Of this I am certain—great fundraisers are most often simply ordinary people who are determined to succeed. They are willing to pay the price. They understand that there are no short-cuts to any place worth going. To anything worth doing. They are committed to integrity fundraising. They aim higher, are more daring, and are willing to give a torrent from their well-spring of time and energy. These become the great ones in finding and keeping.

How certain am I of all this? With apologies to Dr. Seuss:

> I mean all I said,
> I said what I meant—
> I am totally correct,
> One hundred percent.

FASTRACK TENETS

In soliciting for Annual Gifts the Ask drives 80% of getting the gift. The reverse is true of Integrity fundraising. Nurturing (cultivation) is responsible for garnering the major and planned gift. The characteristics of both types of fundraising are depicted below.

ANNUAL FUNDRAISING

Cultivation
Necessary
20%

Ask
80%

INTEGRITY FUNDRAISING

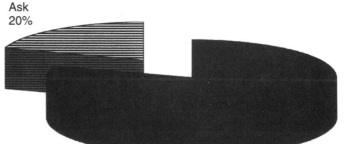

Ask
20%

Cultivation
80%

The Difference Between Annual Giving and Integrity Fundraising

Annual Giving	Integrity Fundraising
For Operating Needs	Usually for Buildings, Endowment, Special Equipment
Sustaining and Regular Gifts	10 to 25 Times Annual Giving
Frequently Asked, Frequently Given	Infrequently Asked, Infrequently Given
Rational, Cerebral Decision	Visceral
Quick Decision	Stop-and-Think Decision
Cash	Pledge, Payments Over an Extended Time
Often Without Spouse	Spouse Involved
Without Professional Assistance	Attorney or Accountant Often Consulted
Direct Mail, Telephone	Personal Solicitation, Likely Several Calls
Leverage Not Critical	Leverage Helps Get the Visit
Alone (Solicitation By One Person)	Several Solicitors

1   Integrity fundraising has little to do with technique. It's all about principles.

2   The fundraiser's job is to: create a clear understanding of the institution's distinct mission . . . and then help the donor feel a high level of urgency about providing the necessary funds to meet that mission.

3   Fundraising is an exchange of values. But it's lopsided. The donor receives much more in value than the actual dollar value of the gift.

4   Fundraising isn't something you do to someone. It's something you do for and with someone.

5   Get to know your prospect. Don't follow any demographic rules. Your prospect is a real person with concerns, needs, pain, and moments of great joy.

6   It is essential that you understand the needs and wants of those you are calling on before you ask for the gift.

7   You develop a trust and rapport before any asking begins. This will likely take a number of visits.

8   You *listen the gift.* You've spent enough time with the person and you have listened carefully enough—that you know precisely the amount you should ask for and the level of interest for the particular project. You know this by listening. If you can't answer the questions about the amount or the interest in the project, you are not ready to ask for the gift.

9   Crafty selling techniques don't work.

10   Develop a high regard, and even an affection, if possible, for the donor. If that type of relationship does not exist—it shows. Don't fake it! Pass the prospect on to a colleague.

11   A fundraiser's high level of integrity will contribute more to the success in achieving a gift than do techniques.

12   Pressure is never to be exerted by the fundraiser. If there is any pressure, it should be imposed by the prospect. They sense the urgency. They understand how their gift can save lives or change lives. They feel the satisfaction of the gift, they anticipate the joy. The pressure is building—the prospect wants or needs to make this gift.

13   In order to enable the donor to make the gift that he or she really wants to make, careful probing is necessary. A *no* does not often mean a *no!* More often it means: *not just yet.*

14 Here's how easy it is:

> The Right Person
>   Asks
> The Right Prospect
>   For
> The Right Amount
>   In
> The Right Way
>   At
> The Right Time
>   With
> The Right Follow-up

2

A Gift From The Duchess

She had perhaps the most arresting features of anyone I've ever met. Certainly not beautiful. Hardly that. Singularly attractive in a somehow surprising way.

I am talking about the Duchess of Windsor. The horrible nightmare that claimed the life of Princess Diana made me think of the Duchess. It brought back memories, nearly twenty years past.

Wait. Don't skip to the next chapter. This isn't still another story about the sordid sovereignty of the British System. This is about fundraising at its highest levels and the lessons I learned.

Read on. This may prove to be of teachable importance to you.

Our firm was involved in a program for the American Hospital of Paris, the first campaign they had ever undertaken. My job, as head of the firm, was to supervise our staff in residence. (It meant going to Paris every four weeks during a two year period. It's a thankless, dull task—but heck, someone had to do it.)

I had a fascinating responsibility. My charge was to be directly and actively involved in the enlistment and solicitation of a number of extraordinary people for the Campaign Advisory Board. Three of the group were particularly noteworthy. There was Guy de Rothschild, Jacqueline Kennedy Onassis, and the Duchess of Windsor.

All three agreed to serve on the Advisory Board, along with a number of other most distinguished and remarkable people.

There's a not a great deal to tell you about the Baron de Rothschild. He made a very sizable gift to the program. And made *faint and charming* contacts with a few of his friends which did not result in gifts.

One day, over lunch, when I asked him how he felt about the American Hospital, he replied: "Ah, the American Hospital is wonderful. It is very special. None of my friends would think of dying anywhere else."

High praise indeed.

Mrs. Onassis did not bring much passion to the Hospital or her board position. When she was recruited, her husband Aristotle's condition was grave. Not long after, he died at the Hospital. The saga of Jacqueline Kennedy Onassis is another story for another time.

But back to the Duchess of Windsor.

I called on her in the glorious residence the French government had provided free to the Duke and Duchess in Bois de Boulogne, a celebrated suburb outside of Paris. She took me on a tour of the château. I counted at least twenty rooms, but I felt there were more. One of her servants, as she referred to them, took my car and a butler met me at the door. I found out later that there was a staff of fourteen assisting in the home.

There I was, sitting in her living room—an unsophisticated, bumbling bumpkin. I felt, as they say, like the fellow who made it possible for the village to have one less idiot.

But there was a graciousness and warmth that I had not expected. She did her best to put me at ease. I can still remember that from sitting where I was, I could see both the Duchess and a life-size, full-scale painting of her on the wall behind. Her presence was enough to give me palpitations. The clone image, virtually a mirror-reflection, made me feel surrounded.

We had a wonderful discussion. She said she would be delighted to serve on the Board. She and the Duke had on many occasions used the American Hospital and they were both indebted to it for past care and courtesies.

Wow, that was easy. It was glorious. I was ready to write psalms.

There wasn't any selling required at all. She was happy to accept. (When I get back to the Hospital, I'll let everyone know about our good fortune and how difficult a job it was recruiting her, and what extraordinary skill I exerted in getting her to accept!)

During the first visit, tea was served. The butler brought a beautiful old sterling biscuit warmer—about twelve inches wide and eight inches high. He carried it with quiet, dignified aplomb. As he was approaching, the Duchess said: "Oh, Mr. Panas wait until you taste these wonderful treats. You will love them." The butler rotated the door and presented me with . . . yes, I was not mistaken—presented me with chitterlings. These are not unknown in some of the poorest regions of the South in our country. I found out later that they are a greatly coveted delicacy in France.

The first question my wife asked when I returned home was: "What was she wearing?" Wives ask those kinds of questions!

I remembered. Of course I remembered. In our business we are trained to absorb and retain every possible detail. I remembered the paintings, the oriental rugs, the tapestries, a gold coat of arms, and photographs. Photographs everywhere. And yes, of course—the glorious jewelry she was wearing.

Most of all, I noticed her suit, a gorgeous powder blue which perfectly matched her eyes. It was a Chanel. I know that because I found out later that Chanel provided all of the Duchess' clothes free. Why not? What a wonderful way to advertise.

There was something else of note. There were three pugs. Now, I don't want to offend any animal lovers, but honestly—does anyone find pugs lovable and huggable dogs?

We were finishing our tea and chitterlings. She was enthusiastic about accepting an appointment on the campaign board. Do I tell her now that this imposes a responsibility to give to the program? Do I dare? What would you have done?

There are two schools of thought on this. Perhaps 22. In any case, two thoughts were racing through my head.

Do I bring up the questions now about giving? We in the business know this issue must be posed, probably sooner than later. Or do I wait until she is more properly warmed to the project, highly cultivated and romanced?

The truth is . . . well, the awful truth is I was afraid to talk with her about money. Let's say hesitant—that sounds better. I was frozen in a state of intimidating awe, just being in the presence of the Duchess. I was certain there would be other opportunities to use my persuasive charms on her.

And there were. There were three more visits. The Duchess is certainly not a warm and comfy person. Hardly. But I noted that, as the visits went on, her austere coldness changed into mild coolness. I considered that a victory of sorts.

The chairman of the campaign was Jacques Maison-rouge, chief executive officer of IBM International. He kept asking how I was coming with the gift from the Duchess. I assured him that we were moving closer and closer.

Have you ever had a prospect you've called on many times . . . and you know you probably should have asked for the gift two visits prior? You keep putting it off. You're afraid of being disappointed, or being turned down, or losing a relationship that meant something to you—more to you, very likely, than the prospect. Maybe it hasn't happened to you. But it was happening to me.

Maisonrouge kept asking. And now the CEO of the Hospital, Perry Cully, was pushing. The moment had finally come. The truth is, I wasn't looking forward to it. Good Grief! I had to ask for the gift.

It was very well known that the Duchess was not a philanthropist. Well, not even a giver. She was a great taker, but not a giver. Had my struggling persistence cracked her shell? Had I spent enough time cultivating? Back then, I hadn't learned what I now preach: Ready, Fire, Aim.

You know full well what I was thinking. I'll wait for one more visit.

That will really warm her up.

But on this fourth visit, which turned out to be the last, we began talking about the responsibilities of a board member. I realized that this was my opportunity, that magic moment I had been waiting for. And dreading. Racing through my mind was every line I had rehearsed, all the words I had taught others to use, the brilliant responses to every possible objection.

I finally blurted out something like: "You wouldn't want to make a gift, would you?"

It wasn't quite that bad, but nearly so.

Well, I had finally said it. Not very well. Quite poorly, in fact. I had violated every rule we teach. But at least the request had been made.

Her face froze into what can only be described as cold marble. "You mean you want me to make a gift to the American Hospital?" I mumbled something about how important her participation would be and how meaningful the support would be to others. I spoke about the responsibility of board members and how she would be a role model for others. I told her about a listing, a plaque we would erect for all to see. I tried to cover every base.

"I'll be back in touch," she said. "I'll let you know." I was glad to get out of the mansion alive.

Now, I know better. I should have gotten a commitment to something. Remember this as being one of the great verities of the solicitation process. When you have made the ask, you must get a commitment to something—if not the gift, at least a new date when you can get together again. I know that now. If I had to live it over again, I would have tried to set a date for another visit. But she was the Duchess and I was still in a deep funk with the inadequate job I had done. She told me that she would be back in touch.

I waited. I waited. In about six weeks, I received an envelope. It had a beautiful gold embossed crest but no identification and no return address. It was unmistakably from the Duchess. I opened it very carefully. I knew this would be a keep-sake.

There was a note with a check. It was very special note which I still have. I keep it in my *Rainy Day File*. The Duchess wrote thanking me for my many visits and the several gifts I had given her—all embarrassingly modest for, after all, what do you give a Duchess?

The check. The check! The check was drawn on a Trust Fund account from a bank in Baltimore. It was for . . . well, I am not going to tell you. Let's just say that it wouldn't have reached the level of the Century Club Circle at the Kokomo, Indiana Community College.

I learned some valuable lessons in all this. Perhaps you have, also.

1   **Board members must give.** I feel now that it is totally acceptable to let a person know that board

membership does impose a gift. It's not off-putting to say something such as: "We'll be talking with you about making a gift to this program. We don't need to discuss it now. Your membership on the board means so very much to us. But on one of my visits soon, I would like to talk with you about what others are doing and what you will likely wish to do for this program."

2   **Know when to send for help.** After the first visit, I should have realized I was well beyond my depth. I was paralyzed in awe of the Duchess. I felt like an acolyte in a room full of bishops. I certainly should have involved a key volunteer. I hadn't because . . . well, because the truth is, I wanted to bring in the gift myself. I wasn't smart enough at the time to realize that I would never be able to win the Duchess by myself. On the other hand, to my credit, there was no one else who felt they were capable of taking her on.

3   **Suggest a specific amount.** I know now that you can not ask for a gift without indicating a specific hoped-for amount. It is the only possible way to know what a person is thinking and if you are seeking at the proper level.

4   **Explore.** After the first or second visit, if you have probed adequately and asked appropriate questions, you should have a pretty good idea of what the person might give. If you don't, you're almost certainly not asking the right questions. In this case, I definitely hadn't.

5   **Non-donors don't normally give.** Don't count on a break-through from a non-donor. Good giving begets better giving. Those who give will give more in the

future. Your largest gifts will come from those who have given in the past. Those who do not have the habit of giving and do not understand philanthropy will seldom make that happy gift you had hoped for. It's like getting the first olive out of the jar. There are surprises, certainly, but not often. In the case of the Duchess, I was wrong to build up my expectation and the hope of others. Don't be guilty of putting yourself in what I call, the *mine-field of expectations.*

6   **Get a commitment to something.** Never leave without getting a commitment to something—the gift or a new date for another visit.

7   **Don't get discouraged.** Treat every disappointment as a learning experience, and get on with it. Move on to your next good prospect. There is a whole world waiting to give. I've learned that an exclusive diet of victories will give you spiritual dyspepsia. It is disappointing to lose once in awhile, but totally acceptable. It happens to all of us. If it hasn't happened to you—you haven't been asking. How can you possibly know the exhilaration and glory of the mountain peak if you have never scrambled through the dredges of a valley.

8   **Examine carefully.** Look critically, objectively at your actions, strategy, and delivery. Be ruthless in your scrutiny. And learn. Be certain you improve and do it better next time. In George Eliot's *Adam Bede,* Mrs. Poyer's stern advise was that, "You must be born again and born different."

9   **Practice.** Asking for a gift is much like a muscle that must be regularly used and exercised to be at its best. Aristotle said: "We are what we repeatedly do. Ex-

cellence, then, is not an act, but a habit." You will improve with practice, but practice that is carefully examined. Remember, "Practice doesn't make perfect. Perfect practice makes perfect."

10 **Relish your experiences.** We are so privileged. We in this field are so favored. We call on wonderful, thoughtful, successful people for glorious causes. Through our efforts, we are directly involved in saving lives and changing lives. Make it an adventure. Be one with Eleanor Roosevelt. She wrote a wonderful book when she was 76 called, *Learn by Living.* She defines her life as an adventure. "My goal was to taste things as fully and as deeply as possible and learn from every experience. There is not a single experience that you can't learn something from."

FasTrack Tenets

1   Board members must give. Why should others give if board members don't?

2   Know when to send for help. You may not be the right person to consummate the gift. Don't worry about who gets the credit. Share the prospect with someone who can be more successful.

3   Always suggest a specific amount when asking for a gift. If you use a range ("I'd like you to consider a gift of $25,000 to $50,000.") the floor becomes the ceiling.

4   Probe, explore, ask questions. It will enable you to *listen the gift*. It's also the only way you can find out if there are any problems or obstacles in the way of getting your gift.

5   Your largest gifts will almost certainly come from those who already give. Good giving begets great giving.

6   After you've asked for a gift, get a commitment to something—either the gift or a date for another meeting.

7   Don't get discouraged. Even the hunter who sits for hours in a clearing will have a deer, sooner or later, cross his path. Be firm, be patient, be positive. There is a world of people waiting for you to ask them for a gift.

8   Review carefully your visit, what you did right, what you would change. Put it in writing. Keep it somewhere handy.

9   Practice, practice, practice. Churchill said: "There is
    nothing that takes me as long to prepare as a spon-
    taneous speech." Be prepared for any eventuality.

10 Learn from your experiences. And, most of all,
    have fun.

3
The *You Can't Miss* System

I was in Houston the other day, working with one of the major medical centers. No city in the nation is quite like the mecca of medical care, research, and innovation as Houston, Texas.

About fourteen board members were around the table discussing the status of fundraising at the institution. I had just completed an assessment of their program, and was admonishing the group about the lack of involvement of volunteers in the fundraising effort. "Here on this board," I said, "are some of the most significant and influential leaders in this community. And you're not using any of this muscle to call on prospects. I don't have a record of any one of you making calls."

One man said: "Are you serious? Do you mean that you really want us calling on people? Are you saying that I should actually ask a person for a gift? Why . . . why . . . my gosh, I wouldn't even know how to begin." This gentleman is the Chief Executive Officer of the General American Life Insurance Company.

I can't believe what I'm hearing. Here's the chief officer of one of the major life insurance companies in the country, a guy who knows a thing or two about selling life insurance. I always thought that selling life insurance took the bravery of one who was willing to walk into a den of lions.

As we went around the table, I heard similar comments from virtually everyone. Here were some of the most prominent people in the community, leaders in their own industry. They were influential leaders, but they all lacked confidence in asking for a gift. I was reminded again that for many, selling a product is quite different, and much easier, than actually asking for a gift.

It doesn't get better. It's not only volunteers. In our seminars for fundraisers I'll often ask: "How many here feel comfortable asking for a gift?" There aren't many hands. Then I ask: "How many here really enjoy asking for a gift?" Even fewer hands. If our professionals have a problem in this area, how can they possibly coach, encourage, and empower volunteers to ask for a gift?

Why We Are Afraid

I'll sometimes run a group through a practice session. "Is anyone here afraid of asking for a gift?" I have a pad handy. I ask them to call out all the reasons they may have for being anxious and apprehensive.

At first they start off slowly. "I'm afraid the person I call on will say no." Or, "I get all choked up." Or, "I can't stand the rejection." Soon, the comments are coming fast and furious. I write as fast as I can, and I keep asking for more and more responses.

The sheets are torn off and placed on a wall. All the fears and anxieties are recorded for all to see. They speak of embarrassment, feelings of failure, and some talk about the disappointment of letting the institution down.

Then I ask what happens if they get a *no*. What happens to them permanently if they are rejected. I start writing down the comments about the permanent damage that is done. There's very little recorded.

It becomes clear. There's no permanent damage when a person is rejected. You can survive rejection. You really can. We talk about how it doesn't feel good and isn't fulfilling. But you can get over it. You don't like the people less who have turned you down. They're wonderful human beings. Life is good. Your spouse loves you. Your dog greets you at the door, wags his tail and wets all over you in joy. Life is still good.

And, finally, I tell them that getting no rejections also means that they're not getting any acceptances. You can't be in the wonderful game of asking for gifts without expecting some disappointments.

Earlier, I wrote about the glory and sacredness of integrity fundraising, the careful nurturing of a person— from prospect to grateful donor. It is a fail-safe process. You can't miss. It is a case of *Tao*. Tao is the eastern religious term designating the unwavering course from which one cannot deviate. You must be one with T.S. Eliot who, in his *Four Quartets*, says that you can go to the village of Little Gidding from wherever you are. But you must know what your destination is. *If you come this way, taking the route you would be likely to take, from the place you would be likely to come from—you will assuredly find it.*

But my world is different. At the most, I have only two calls I can make on a prospect. Sometimes more, but very, very seldom. And that's the world of most of the campaigns I'm involved in. If you can get a volunteer to make one call, you consider yourself fortunate. Two calls is sublime. Heaven has graced you. More than that is unrealistic.

Let me tell you what I like to do on my calls. Don't use my words. They work for me, but they may feel awkward to you or may not flow trippingly off your tongue. It's the concept I want you to hear.

But first let me tell you about a study we conducted. The study is important because it explains everything there is to know about how I make my contacts and why I do what I do.

When you or volunteers make a contact, the prospect almost always knows that you're calling for a gift. There may be exceptions, but not many. In fact, there is virtue in knowing that a request is going to be made. Otherwise, you may stand the chance of cardiac arrest when you mention the amount you're asking. Personally, I think it's a matter of civility in letting a person know that it's not a social call or an inquiry about their health.

What Focus Groups Told Us

We conducted a number of Focus Groups to determine how people felt about being asked for a gift, who they liked calling on them, the kind of material they liked to see, and that sort of thing. We posed questions like: *You know that they have come to call on you for a gift. How does that affect your thinking during the presentation? What thoughts are going through your mind during the presentation? Do you like a written proposal? Do you like to be asked for a specific dollar amount?* It wasn't precisely that, but that will give you an idea of how we frame the questions in each group.

The responses were fascinating. And I suspect they won't surprise you a great deal. The kind of comments that follow were rather typical:

> "When they started talking, I didn't hear a thing they said. I kept thinking about how much they were going to ask me for."

> "I knew they had come to ask me for a gift. I kept wondering how much they were going to ask for. I kept thinking, how am I going to get out of this?"

> "I tried to concentrate on what they were saying, but it was difficult. I knew they've come to ask for a gift and I had a feeling that they had put me down for much more than I was planning to give. I was wondering how to get out of this without being embarrassed."

None of that is necessarily negative. But it occurred to me, as if in a revelation, that you do not have the complete concentration of the person you're talking to, no matter how dazzling your presentation. Their thoughts are wrapped entirely around the amount you are going to ask for.

I guess I always thought that this was the case, but now I had research to back it up. That's when I began changing my approach. Mind you, in my world I only have two contacts I can make, perhaps three. Very seldom more than that. I don't have the opportunity for the kind of nurturing fundraising I described earlier.

After our research, this is what I started doing in my contacts. After the greeting and gaining some sort of rapport, I'd say something such as: *Mrs. Noyes, I've come today to ask you for $100,000. Let me tell you how we're going to use the money and how your gift can make the difference.* I figured that by coming right out with the amount, I wouldn't keep the prospect wondering about how much I was going to ask for.

I know that sort of an introduction works for some people, but I kept gagging on it. Somehow it wasn't right for me. If it feels good to you, use it. I give it to you as a present.

Here's what I do now instead. I commend it to you. And in my training sessions with volunteers, I also suggest that they try it. I used it just the other day for a major university in the southeast. I had a great advantage. In this case, I was calling on someone who loved the university.

We exchanged pleasantries and established some common ground. I reminded him (in a subtle way, I hope) of his love for the university and his indebtedness to the institution (he went through on a scholarship). And then I said something such as:

Jim, I've come today to talk with you about the university and its vision for the future. There is a project in particular that I want to discuss— it's something I think you're going to be terribly excited about. (And now, my voice volume increases a bit, barely perceptible but enough that it gives it emphasis.) *I am not going to ask you for a gift today. We are not even going to discuss money. I just want to tell you about this exciting project. But I'm coming back, and when I do, I'm going to ask you for a great deal of money. But not today.*

Here's what I believe it does for the session. I haven't tested it empirically, but the results have been so good that I am confident I am on target. That kind of a statement shifts the gears from reverse to neutral. We are ready to begin. I'm not facing any blocks, no hurdles I have to jump over, no worries about my asking for an embarrassing amount. Jim's hands are out of his pockets. He's not clutching his money.

We talk about the enticing program. I see that Jim is finding parts of it irresistible. I probe, I question, I test for concerns. I do all of those things which I will describe a bit later.

We get to that bewitching moment when you would normally ask for a gift. Instead, I use a close much as I did with Jim.

> *Jim, it's been wonderful having the time with you. And I can see that you're really interested in this program. I was certain you would be. Pull out your calendar, I want to set a time for another visit.* (Note that I did not call it an appointment. I'll explain that small matter to you later.)

> Almost always, the person I'm talking with will say: *Aw, come on—there's no need to set up another date. We can talk about the money today. It's okay. I know that you have something in mind.* Jim followed that pattern. That's almost precisely what he said.

> My response is typically something such as: *Jim, we didn't have anything really in mind for you. But for a program such as this, I thought you would want to make a gift of $1 million.* (Note, I didn't say that we thought he should make a gift, or the horrible statement that we had him down for $1 million. That's really a killer!) I said that I was pretty certain that he would want to make a gift of this size. We negotiated, we talked some more, and he raised some valid concerns. In the end, it did take another visit.

I sent Jim a very special thank-you for the visit. And I made certain that the chancellor of the University sent a letter of appreciation, also, indicating *how helpful and thankful Jerry felt about the fine session.*

I call this my *Not Today* approach. It works for me.

Now I want to present an outline of how to make an ask, the steps you take in actually asking for the gift. Nothing is guaranteed. As they say, it's about as fail-proof as having your home guarded by a cat. But these steps cover every base. You can proceed with total confidence and complete comfort. You're on your way. As Phillip Lopate says about Seneca's writing: "The results could be both dazzling and fatiguing."

Asking for the gift is clearly an art form. That's why *Rules and Hoary Verities* do not hold up very well. The basic common denominators are well established, but there are many applications and interpretations, detours along the way that seem to go on forever and lead finally to the road to nowhere.

I find that the difference between the outstanding fundraisers and those who do not do as well is not the workshops and seminars they attended, or the knowledge they have acquired—but rather how they use that information to achieve their objectives.

Experience counts. You will do far better the more calls you make, you will understand that there are no pat answers—only helpful suggestions to point you in the right direction. And you understand that the quest is unending.

Neil Rackaham, in his classic book, *Spin Selling,* talks about *entelechy*—the phenomenon of making actual that which only before was potential. That, it seems to me is what our job is all about. It is reputed that Ghandi said: "If you don't ask, you don't get." I have a difficult time believing that Ghandi really said that. But the sentiment is right on target. But take Wayne Gretzky, the great hockey player. Now there's someone who knows what he's talking about. He says: "I miss 100% of the shots I never take."

You're ready for your coaching session. (Note, I don't call it *training*. I want you to be able to use this with your volunteers, and volunteers don't like to be *trained*. They don't mind being coached. That seems like a small difference, but in this business, God is in the trifles. If you don't believe me, just try it. Send out a notice for a Training Meeting, and your volunteers, even the dedicated ones, will stay away in droves. It's a case of *include me out*.)

Would you like to know why you won't get the gift? As you can imagine, we did some studies regarding this, also. We are, after all, in the business of raising funds. After you complete this chapter, none of the following can happen to you—but here's what we found.

Reasons You Didn't Get The Gift

Inadequate Preparation. You didn't take time to prepare, to know your donor, or to practice. You went dashing into the session thinking, *I'll make the call and get it over with*. You got the kind of results you deserve.

Anxiety. You were nervous, insecure, and uneasy. It was not *an easy* session, and it showed. Chances are, if you were properly prepared and had practiced, you could have overcome all of this.

Assuming Too Much. You called on someone whom you felt knew a good bit more about the institution and the project than was actually the case. You jumped to the close too soon because you assumed too much. Or you called on someone who had been actively involved in the institution over a period of years. You took for granted that they would be interested in the project. No need to interpret, to sell the dream, to discuss how important their gift would be. That's what you thought. You asked for the gift too soon—you leaped from step one to step nine. You lose.

Failure to Probe. The prospect was nodding in approval and smiling throughout your entire bold presentation. You left thinking you had made the case, made the sale. You failed to examine for any concerns, probe for any biting questions. If you don't probe, you haven't even begun to make the ask.

Poor Listening. You talked too much, you listened too little. You never had an opportunity to find out how the prospect felt about the program because you were spending all of your time talking. You failed to *listen the gift*.

Too Much on Features, Not Enough on Benefits. You spent your time going over details and speaking about features (the gymnasium will be regulation size, the new center will have nine Conference Rooms, and that sort of thing) and not enough time talking about how the program would save lives or change lives. You missed your golden opportunity.

Premature Selling. You asked for the gift and made a brilliant close—but you hadn't taken time to make the program properly irresistible. You hadn't probed for concerns or listened. You raced from first to third base, without touching second.

Win-Win. You spent all of your time talking about how important the program was for the institution and how it would meet its needs. You didn't talk about those who would be served. More important, you didn't talk about how it would benefit the donor. It's got to be a win-win.

To provide the funds to meet your mission, you and your volunteers need to call on a number of people. The key to getting everything you need is never to put all of your begs in one ask-it. You need to have a strong base, a significant foundation.

You can help determine those who are the most likely you should call on by going through electronic screening. This is very possibly the most effective way to begin, and probably the most scientific. Another, less scientific but helpful way is to use **FLAG**. Using this system will help you review your donor base to determine who should be called on earliest for major gifts.

Frequency: The number of gifts that have been made.

Length: The number of years the person has been giving to the institution.

Affinity: The depth of involvement the person has had in activities of the organization.

Giving: The size of the gifts in the past.

Use this system. It works. It is as systematic as electronic screening. It will not pinpoint those who have the high capacity for giving, but it will indicate among your constituency who are the most likely to make a large gift. You will be able to **FLAG** them. Now we're ready for our coaching session.

Let's assume that we're working with a group of volunteers. This will be as effective one-on-one with a volunteer, but it really works far better in a group. I've done plenty of the knee-to-knee coaching, one-on-one. But there's no excitement, no interplay, no passion. I've also done it with a group of 400 volunteers and I felt the energy and enthusiasm lifting me off the platform.

1   I start by telling the group to begin by reviewing all of the material in their kit. This often includes the campaign brochure and any ancillary material that has to do with the program. Maybe the most current Annual Report, or other program folders.

      I also like to include written tips and suggestions on how to most effectively make a call. We are going to review all of that in our coaching session, but having it in writing as something they can review is extremely helpful. Hey, this is tough stuff for volunteers—they need all the help they can get.

      I also like to include what is typically called a Question & Answer piece. Usually, this is printed in a fairly basic and simple way, perhaps with a photo or two and some graphs. I consider it the most effective piece in the material arsenal. It is no nonsense, straight, and concise—and that is precisely what makes it so effective.

Here's how to do a Q & A folder. Start with a small group of volunteers and a staff person or two. Think of the 15 or 20 questions that are most likely to be asked. Some of these will be sensitive, some of them may even be embarrassing or awkward. But these are the questions that your prospects will be thinking about or asking directly. There needs to be an effective answer. Take that longer list and hone it to the 8 or 10 questions that you feel will be the most penetrating and basic. Those that you are fairly certain will be on the minds of those you contact. Take that smaller group of questions and ask the best writer you have to respond. You'll need to work with this person, of course. Make the case and substantiate your response.

I remember a campaign in Evanston, Illinois. The case was the least dramatic and appealing that you could possibly present. We had indicated that the project would cost $21 million. After the bids came in, we discovered that there was a fall-short of $7 million. Our architect had simply underestimated what it would cost to build.

We somehow had to explain this to our constituency—how it was possible to miss the cost by that much. It was complicated by the fact that we were using a local, well-known, and highly regarded architect. We did not want to make him out to be the fool. Still, we had to explain why we were coming back immediately for $7 million.

The question in the folder was something such as: *How could you possibly have miscalculated by $7 million?* Our response in the answer section was:

We goofed!

There was something about this response that really did the job. It was clear. It was concise. And it took the curse off of being defensive. We went on to explain how it is possible to make that kind of an error. But the admission was so disarming, it seemed to do the trick.

A question and answer piece is a great tool for your workers and for those you call on.

2   I then tell our group to review the prospects' giving and activity history. Everything we can give in the way of background information is critically important.

Some question whether it is proper (breaking faith with the person being called on) to provide all of the data on how much has been given in the past. I err on the side of giving as much information as we possibly can. That includes any giving we know about to other institutions. The more you can arm your volunteers with, the better.

It's important for the worker to know everything there is about the person, the couple, he or she is calling on. Every bit of information is important. Whether they have served on the board in the past, whether they have participated in any activities, whether any of their children have been involved, and so on. Everything counts.

3   Be clear about how much you should ask for. I am firm on this—I tell my volunteers to ask for a specific amount. Do not ask for a range. Not asking for

a specific amount is comparable to starting on a trip without knowing where you are going.

There's a risk in all of this. No matter how often you tell your volunteers to be careful about not saying to a person something such as: "We've got you down for $25,000"—some will blurt it out. It happens. It's a case of nervousness, anxiety, not knowing how else to express the request. I'll refer later on to the magic words that transform a presentation into your request.

Explain to your volunteers how you came up with the amount you're suggesting. I say something such as this:

You know, in order to determine that we could raise the funds we need to complete this project, we had to make certain that there was the giving capacity within our family and those who care about us. We had to make that sort of an evaluation to be sure that we can raise the money we need to make this happen. That meant that we simply had to take a good look at all of our prospects to see if we had the capacity. So here's what we did: We enlisted three or four people who know our group really well. I won't tell you who they are! But they met for hours and hours and hours. It's not an easy job. They were very careful about each person they evaluated. They didn't try to be conservative and they were careful not to be off the wall. They really worked at being realistic. I think you will find these numbers pretty much on target.

(By the way, this is a great way to use the **FLAG** assessment. Have your small group that does the evaluations use it.)

Frequency

Loyalty

Affinity

Giving

Better still **PEG**—**P**rospect **E**valuation **G**rid—all of your prospects. The **PEG** is as accurate a barometer as I've seen to gauge the giving of your prospects. I have included the instrument in the Appendix.

> *You may know something about these people we don't. We may have aimed too low—and because of some things that you know, we should really ask for more. Or perhaps there are some expenses or mitigating situations that are happening now that makes our ask-figure too high. We need to know that.*

Each person has a *Gift Card* with the person's name and information on it. Everything is there. The asking figure is not on this card—it's with the data on the prospect that is kept with the solicitor.

4   This will seem like a small matter, but we now call these *Gift Cards*. Several years ago, I stopped calling these prospect cards, or what is more normally called, Pledge Cards. *Gift* has a very positive connotation. *Pledge* does not.

In fact, we have changed the language on our cards to make certain that the prospect knows that they are not legally binding. Instead of the legal language, we use something such as:

I/We believe so strongly in the work of the Middletown Community Hospital and the need for a new Cardiac Center, it is our intention over the next three years to give $_____ . It is our understanding that this is not a legally binding pledge and that it will not encumber our estate. We shall, of course, make every effort to fulfill this intention. But it is clear that if there is any reason at all why we cannot, we shall notify the Hospital . . .

Our experience is that an indication of the *intention* is a much more positive way of getting the investment.

Have you've been through it as often as I have—that a person does not want to make a legally binding pledge: "I never make pledges." Or: "I don't know what it will be like for me next year." Or: "I don't want this kind of gift to be taken out of my estate."

Our *Words of Intention* take the curse off of all that. There is such greater spirit and enthusiasm for making a gift of this sort.

5   Tell your volunteers now to give some thought as to how they will express the amount they are going to ask for. Some have never asked for a gift of $10,000 or $25,000, while others have never asked for a gift at all. It can be a moment of sheer terror. I say to the group, *Repeat after me: fifty thousand dollars.* I ask them to repeat it, but this time with much more enthusiasm: Fifty thousand dollars! I tell them how

wonderful they are and how easy it was for them to say it.

For those who haven't solicited often, they can gag when it comes to the moment when they are to ask for a gift. This happens even to some who do it often—the tongue gets thick, the mouth gets dry, they feel they have a chicken bone stuck in their throat.

6   Make certain that each of your volunteers knows that they can call the chief executive officer and the chief development officer at any time. At any time! I like listing the private line into their office and the home telephone number. Yes, the home number. You say that you put your foot down at some point. No home calls! Okay, okay. That's up to you. I like to have my volunteers know that the staff is accessible to them at any time.

7   Get ready for the next step. It represents eighty-five percent of getting the gift. That's how important it is.

I'm talking about making the call to get the *visit*. (Note, I do not call it *an appointment*. This will seem like a small matter to some—but calling for a *visit* has a very positive ring to it. A *visit* is something you do with friends.)

8   Setting the visit can be tough. I know how difficult it can be. I have been there myself. I've been doing this a long time but there are some contacts where I still go through the telephone heebie-jeebies.

Have you ever done this? You stare at the telephone for ten full minutes. You know that at some point, you have to punch in the numbers. But you live in high hope that somebody will call you and the telephone will ring. You have escaped. You don't have to make the dreaded call.

But the phone doesn't ring and you realize that you do indeed have to make the call. But it's easier than you think. I promise. Much like what Mark Twain said about Wagner's music: *It's not as bad as it sounds.*

There's a fine line between being prepared and sounding down-pat. Being prepared means you know what you're talking about—but you're able to make it sound as if you were saying it for the first time. If you recite your lines as if by rote, it is deadly. You have all had those kinds of telephone calls yourself.

9   Have a calendar handy. Remember, you're making the call to set a date. The telephone in one hand, the pencil and a calendar by your side.

10   Practice, practice, practice. It's all right to go through a script. Remember, it has to be down-pat but it should still sound spontaneous! Keep in mind Churchill's admission: "I have to practice a great deal in order to make a speech sound spontaneous." It's worth the time and effort to practice. Keep in mind that getting a visit puts you eighty-five percent on your way to getting the gift.

11   I like sending a note in advance alerting the prospect that I'll be calling to set a time for a visit. Explain in the letter your involvement in the program and the purpose of the call. There are those who feel that such a letter for some will be a warning—and will

permit them to come up with reasons why they don't want to see you. I find just the opposite. The note is a courtesy and enables you to get right into your telephone call without spending time to explain the reasons you want to see them.

Do you indicate that you are going to talk about the project? I do.

Do you indicate in the note that you are going to ask about a gift? Actually, quite the opposite. Remember the *Not Today* concept I described earlier. I use that somewhat in the note:

I am not going to ask you for a gift, not on this visit. What I want to do is talk about our program and how much I believe it will mean to you.

12   That moment has come. You're ready to make the call. Break the ice, but don't spend a great deal of time on meaningless conversation. Your purpose is to set the date.

Hello, John. This is Jerry Panas. You perhaps know how deeply involved I am with the program for The Salvation Army. I want to bring you up to date on some of the things that we're doing and invite you to join us in the program. Is Tuesday or Wednesday next week the better day for us to get together?

I like to give two choices of dates. I can negotiate from there if necessary for a different time, but I find that giving two dates provides a choice. It seems to work better. But sometimes you run into a problem.

Jerry, I'm not sure it's a good idea for us to get together. I don't believe I want to get involved in the

campaign program. I contribute to the Annual Fund, but I'm not interested in doing more.

You hope for better, but it doesn't always happen the way you want it. You could leave it at that, thank the person for his or her consideration, and go on to the next prospect. But you know better. You know that it is going to take a personal visit to get a gift at the level you want. And you know that your cause is so important and so many lives are involved, that you have to exert yourself. This isn't easy. You'd prefer having your teeth scraped, but you go on.

John, it's important that I see you. I promise that the choice to be involved is entirely yours. I'm not a good enough salesman to change your mind about doing something that you don't want to do. But this program is the most important in our history. All I'm asking for is an opportunity to invite you into the partnership with us. I understand that you may have to evaluate circumstances. But you know me well enough to know that you can be honest with me and I'll respect whatever you decide. What time is better for you next week, Tuesday or Wednesday?

There, you did it. It wasn't easy, but you did it.

Jerry, just tell me how much you're looking for. Maybe we can accomplish this all on the telephone. I really don't have much time. And I'm not crazy about fundraising and being asked.

This isn't getting any easier. What's the old Chinese torture—having your toenails pulled? I think I'd prefer going for that. But instead I say something such as this:

I just don't feel comfortable, John, trying to handle this on the telephone. It's too important. Look, I'm willing to give it thirty minutes if you can give me that much time, also. Will you do that for me? Will you give me thirty minutes? What is going to be better for you, Tuesday or Wednesday? We can get over the business quickly and then go on to lunch.

What happens if you're still swimming upstream, the tide against you? Your prospect says:

Look, why don't you just send me all of the information. I promise to look it over and I'll send you a check.

I'd take one more shot.

Knowing you as I do, I really believe that you would give it a careful reading and very likely send a check. And I want you to know how important that would be to us and to me personally. But, the material simply can't convey the importance and excitement of this program. I really believe it is something that will interest you. I know how busy you are, but I'm willing to match my time with yours. When can I come to see you?

These are just a few of the stiff-arms that you can get. I don't even call them objections. They are the kind of responses you should expect. This is important: Before you make your telephone calls, come up with a list of the concerns or objections that you might get. Then write down the kind of response you will give. And practice. Every situation will be different and that will mean different kinds of responses. For instance:

Jerry, I already give so much. You know I've been giving to them for years.

John, I know that. In fact, that's one of the reasons I'm calling on you. You have been such a great friend to us over the years. It's our friends that we are calling on now for this important program.

13   Keep in mind, your job is to get the visit. It is not to make the case, as much as your prospect may try to corner you into doing it.

Listen, Jerry, why don't you tell me what this is all about. We could probably do a lot of this on the telephone. Tell me why you're coming to see me.

It's a great project, John. The truth is, I couldn't do it justice on the telephone. I have a feeling this is something that you're really going to be interested in, and I have some photographs and material I want to share with you, also. You're going to find this important. When is a good time to meet you next week—Tuesday or Wednesday?

And, keep in mind, you are not to solicit on the telephone—as much as your prospect may try to move you in that direction.

We're both so busy, Jerry. I know you're coming to talk with me about a gift but I think we can handle this on the telephone—and save us both some time. Why don't you just begin telling me about it now?

I know this is something that is going to interest you, John, and that's why I'm so keen on visiting you in person. I don't feel I can do justice to the program on the telephone, and I think we would both lose if I at-

tempted that. I know how busy you are. If you weren't so busy, you wouldn't be as successful as you are. The folks I'm calling on are all terribly busy and that's why I've been careful about the time I take. I'm certain that we can wrap all of this up in thirty minutes. I'm hoping that you'll give me that much time. When is a good day for a visit next week, Tuesday or Wednesday?

There's another suggestion I offer to volunteers that seems to get good results. They tell me that it often turns the prospect around. It goes something such as this:

I know how busy you are, John. That's one of the reasons I'm so eager to see you. You're the kind of person that gets things done. The truth is, I really didn't want to take on this assignment. I'm not very keen on fundraising. It's not something I look forward to. I finally said I'd be willing to do it because I think it's so darn important. When Stanley, the chairman of the campaign, finally got me to take this on, I promised that I would call on all of those I was assigned to. I made that commitment. And you're one of the important ones I feel I really must see.

14   Be patient, be firm, be positive. No one said it would be easy. You'll find that the letter I suggested prior to the telephone call will help. It will grease the way.

I find it sometimes helps to have a *door opener* write the pre-telephone call letter for you. That's a person who knows your prospect as well, or perhaps even better than you do, and is at a level that is very difficult to say *no* to. It's really worth the time and effort to determine who should write that letter.

I was reminded of a board meeting in Omaha for The Salvation Army. We were reviewing the names of our top prospects. One name came up that was certain to be a sizable gift if we could only get to see him. The problem was that no one knew him well enough to make a strong connection. One board member, trying to be helpful, said: *I was the best man at his third wife's first wedding.* Somehow, I didn't think that would be helpful! Find just the right person who can open the door for you.

15 I'm a great advocate of calling in pairs, particularly on the first visit. I call it *The Magic Partnership.* That's when a volunteer with some leverage goes with a staff person, the chief executive officer or the development staff, to make the call. The one has the influence and the other has all of the information. We find that those who make really sizable gifts want to talk to a staff person who is knowledgeable and can interpret the vision of the institution.

More and more, I'm finding major donors are insisting that they talk to staff. They may be impressed with the board and feel good about what they know about the institution—but they are keenly interested in getting inside the heads of those who make the organization run.

Claude Rosenberg is the author of *Wealthy and Wise.* It's a book you must read and put in the hands of chief volunteers and top donors. He is a significant philanthropist. He told me that he won't make a major gift unless he speaks to the chief executive officer. Most major donors I talk with these days feel the same.

All of the reasons you think of for going in pairs make it a good idea. You carefully work out the scenario and determine who will say what, who will lead, and who will finally make the ask. All of that is prepared and practiced. Going in pairs provides a change of pace, a change of voice, and an opportunity for the solicitors to bounce things back and forth and catch their breath. And if one stumbles, the other picks it up.

There's another important benefit. I find in many situations, the volunteer can make an absolutely eloquent presentation, compelling and dramatic. But when it comes to making the ask, they somehow lose their voice. This is a good place for the staff to step in to help his partner who is choking and reaching for a glass of water.

There's another real advantage that comes later, on the second or third visit if these are necessary. If a good transfer is made, the staff person (or the volunteer) can pick it up easily and make all of the other visits. You need not go again in pairs.

16   Ahh, you have the date for your visit. In some ways, it really wasn't as difficult as you thought. And it didn't follow the script exactly, did it? I tried to prepare you as effectively as I could, but there are always questions and roadblocks that are thrown in your way.

Instead of speeding down some boring interstate of coaching, paved by research and previous campaigns, your call took a detour through some strange and forbidding landscapes. Some of you are reminded that Janet Leigh would never have met Anthony Perkins at the Bates Motel had she not turned off the highway. It can happen. But most of the time you're on your way to a wondrous time and a glorious visit. You are eighty-five percent on your way to getting the gift. Someone once asked Ben Hogan what is the most crucial shot in golf. Hogan said: "The one you're about to hit."

17   You are with your prospect. Establish a rapport and a common ground. There's no magic to the amount of time this should take. Take whatever is necessary. Just be certain that this doesn't dominate your session and steal from your clear mission—to get the gift.

Talk about how you both care and how you are both dedicated to the work and service of the organization. If it's an alumna of a university, it's easy to talk to her about the school. If it's a fellow parent and you both have children going to the school, it's easy to talk about how you are both dedicated to the school. But if you're talking to a prospect and you're not quite certain how great his or her interest might be—you need to probe with some open questions.

We've talked a little bit about the YMCA and the impact it's making in our community. I told you about some of their programs in the inner-city where I feel they are touching the lives of young people in a way no other organization does. As we were talking, it seemed to me that you are quite concerned about the need for work in the inner-city. How important do you feel this is? How do you feel about the role of the YMCA and what they are doing?

Note that these are indirect queries. Questions such as these cannot be answered *yes* or *no*.

18 It's essential that you probe for concerns. Use open questions. If you do not understand how the prospect truly feels about the institution, you will know nothing about your progress in the solicitation. If you spend all of your time talking instead of listening, you'll uncover no new information. Probe. Examine. Question.

I remember several years ago when I was making a call with a volunteer for a major campaign for the hospital in Salisbury, Maryland. We had scripted it fairly well and the volunteer, Fulton, knew that he was to ask and probe. Fulton began the call by asking the prospect how he felt about the hospital. His response was something like this: "It's a horrible place. I think the medical staff stinks. The nursing care is terrible. When I was in there, they didn't have anyone on the floor who spoke English. The place is filthy." It would not have been appropriate for us to say something such as: "Thank you for sharing that helpful information!"

Fulton was quick: "Ben, I am embarrassed that I thought I knew you so well that I felt you loved the hospital and would be interested in this program. I am obviously wrong. Tell me a little bit more about what happened on your visit so we can get to the bottom of this."

Ben went on, nonstop, for the next fifteen or twenty minutes. He finally wound down. And then something very special happened. When he got it all out of his system, he seemed to feel much better. It's as if he had been waiting and waiting for someone to talk to about the hospital. Finally he said: "Well, maybe it wasn't as bad as I've made out. And we certainly need a good hospital in Salisbury. What did you want to talk with me about?" We went on to get the gift.

The secret was Fulton's thoughtful manner in which he handled the complaint and his ability to listen with interest and concern. How did I feel when Ben first registered the complaint? I'll tell you how I felt. It was very much like wrestling with the giant Briareos, with his hundred arms and his fifty heads, all of them shouting and laughing, and grabbing at me. That's how I felt. You know what it's like, too. You've been there yourself.

It's worth repeating that when talking to a person, you tune the world out and the other person in. You work hard at putting people completely at ease and making them feel important. You get them talking about themselves and their concerns. You probe. You hold eye contact and you listen to how they feel. And you understand fully that (in the early stages especially) people are more likely to listen to you later if you are listening to them.

19 Conversation is essential because it gives you an opportunity to listen. Questions are essential because you're able to uncover any concerns or issues that might exist.

20 Finally you are at that moment. You are about to present the great opportunity. You have come to that point in the visit where you explain the great opportunity. You take no more than eleven minutes.

Let me explain the eleven minutes. Oh, certainly, I suppose you can take more if necessary. But not much. All of the research indicates that this is about the maximum time a person can handle without tuning you out. You can be the best judge as you are talking with your prospect, but be careful.

I'll give you a good analogy that helps explain my position in this regard. When you plan a video, the producer will tell you that it must not be any longer than 8 to 12 minutes. There's good reason for that. They understand that a video cannot hold a person's attention for any longer than that time. But think about it. The video has a great deal going for it. There's a musical background. There's something always flashing in the background. It has professional narration. There's sound effects. Heck, it's like a gypsy wedding. And with all of this going for it, your video must not take more than 8 to 12 minutes. So, if your dazzling asking presentation can be that inspiring, you may take more time—but be forewarned.

21   It doesn't always happen, but if you can have a volunteer working with you who is head-over-heels devoted to your institution, you're well on your way to getting the gift. You hope for a volunteer who has the same passion for the organization as they do for their hobby. If they feel that passion, commitment, and joy—they will be unbeatable. You hope for a man or woman who will turn their volunteerism into their vocation. It will become their way of life, their ministry. They will live and breathe the institution and fundraising. Take a volunteer who is burning in their bones for the organization.

22　In discussing the opportunity with the prospect, it's not enough to talk about how the gift will benefit the institution and those who are served. It is essential to convey the benefit to the donor. Discuss how many lives this program will change and save—and how this intersects with the life of the donor. You can discuss the joy the gift will bring to the donor, the recognition, and the sense that they are indeed directly saving lives. To get the largest gift possible, it has to be a win-win situation—for the institution and the donor.

23　Be careful not to make the size of the gift dominate the presentation. Make it secondary to determining what most effectively fills the needs of the prospect.

You're not trying to manipulate the donor and you understand that tricky negotiations are repugnant.

You emphasize an exchange of values. You have identified problems and objections, and you have responded so that this is a win-win situation. You have determined and eliminated the roadblocks. In a sense, asking for a gift is creative problem-solving, not manipulation.

It is certainly not fast-talking, outsmarting, out-gimmicking your prospect. It's working out the best solution for both the donor and the institution. You understand full well that you are helping the prospect to make an investment that will bring joy and satisfaction, that will help save lives and change lives.

24　Don't sell features. Talk about outcomes. Here's something else I have found helpful. It may seem insignificant, but I have found it works. When I am talking about features or referring to the campaign material, it is all right to call attention or point to the folders or the features. But when you are talking about benefits and how this will touch the lives of those who are served, that's where the real sale takes place. You rivet your attention. You look directly at the person.

25   The case for your program must have relevancy, drama, and emotional appeal. Most of all, there must be a high sense of urgency. These few factors must exist and must be interpreted in your presentation.

I try to shy away from talking about big, abstract numbers. I don't feel that the fact that we have an all-time high of 11,000 students is very dramatic. And that we served 50,000 in the emergency room is not very compelling. Nor that there are 3,000 homeless in the streets of our city.

I like to think of what I call *The Anne Frank Concept*. It's hard to conceive of the six million children who died in the Holocaust. But it's easy to get completely overwhelmed in the Anne Frank story. When making a presentation, I think *Anne Frank*.

I've stopped using blue prints in my presentations. Where's the excitement and drama in that? Sure, if you're calling on an engineer or a builder, have the blueprints handy. But most people won't be able to follow you through them. I've lost many a prospect on my way down a corridor of a blue print.

Creating a sense of urgency is key. Unless the need is pressing and immediate, why should the prospect give? Many other worthwhile programs are calling for their help. And why should they be concerned about making a timely decision? If the need isn't dire, there's no urge to make a decision.

26   Now comes what I consider to be one of the most telling and effective parts of the presentation. Assuming you have a volunteer involved in the call, the volunteer gives testimony to his or her gift. If you're the staff making the call, give testimony to what others have done (with their permission, of course) and why.

This is a good point to remind you that you should never use a volunteer to make calls on your behalf unless they have made a gift themselves. I like to ask the volunteer to make *a sacrificial gift*—but for some, that may seem too challenging and hairy. Let's just say that you want your volunteer to give at a level that makes them stand on tip-toes. Giving testimony to their own gift confirms the importance of the program. Best of all, it also provides another opportunity to talk about the importance of the project.

Giving testimony is a powerful tool. That's why it's so important that the volunteer has made a gift, and at the proper level. I remember a call I made early in my career. I was with a volunteer, and he had made an excellent presentation. When he was finished and had asked for the gift, the prospect asked him: "This seems like something I would be interested in. How much have you given to the project?" That's a fair enough question. I can assure you that even if it isn't asked, it's something the prospect would like to know. It's one way of gauging the appropriateness of the ask. In this case, the volunteer said: "Well . . . I haven't made up my mind yet. We're still thinking about it." The prospect was very upset. "Why don't we finish this off now. And when you make up your mind and decide what you're going to give, come back and see me." I'll never make that mistake again.

And let me tell you what happened with Claude Rosenberg, one of the great spirits of San Francisco Philanthropy. He was called on by the chairman of the board of Goodwill Industries. It was, according to Rosenberg, "a great presentation, something I was really interested in.

"It didn't hurt, either, that the chairman was a good friend of mine. I had invested a great deal of money for him and he had done well. He is very, very wealthy.

"So I tell him that I'm really interested in the program. He had asked me for $500,000, and in this case this sounded reasonable. So I asked him how much he had given. And he tells me he had given $500,000.

"I told him that I wouldn't even consider a gift, certainly not at that level. For one thing, I knew what he was worth, and it's many times more than me. But even more important, as chairman of the organization, he is supposed to lead the way. He is supposed to set the pattern. There's no way that I was going to equal his gift. It's his organization, not mine."

Here's an example of how your volunteer might give testimony to his or her gift:

I'm going to ask you, John, to share with me in this program but before I do, let me tell you what Felicity and I decided to give to the project. We're giving $50,000. You know us pretty well and you know that will really stretch us. It's the largest gift we've ever given to anything. Let me tell you why we decided to do that. We thought about it for a long time, we discussed it, and you know—we even prayed about it. We decided that this program was so important because of . . .

27   You've come to that moment. See, it wasn't that hard. You've probed. You've asked questions. You've listened. You presented a dramatic and urgent opportunity, and you've given testimony to your own gift. Now you're ready to transform your entire visit into the ask for the gift. The words I use to make it easiest for me are fairly simple:

I would like you to consider a gift of . . .

That's how easy it is. Not much magic to all of that. Simply: *I would like you to consider . . .*

The next point is very important. You have asked for the gift. Don't fill in the silence. You wait for the prospect to speak. It will seem like hours. It's what I call the loud and deafening silence. There are times that I felt it was so long I could be excused to go for a walk. But you resist the temptation—you don't talk. If you do, you may never know how the prospect really feels about the program and the gift.

28   In a sense, the negotiating now begins. How carefully do you feed a 700-pound gorilla—as carefully and as well as possible. Your objective is to secure

the largest gift possible—but no larger than will benefit to the greatest extent the donor's interest and intent. You have gauged your ask accordingly. It has to be a win-win situation.

29 You don't get rattled by objections. It may sound trite, but objections are indeed your best friends. If you don't know how the prospect truly feels, you won't know what you have to overcome. Your job is to respond—to propose and dispose, but not impose and oppose. You don't prevail, knock down, and win. You resolve objections.

You show no sign of arrogance or hostility. You remain patient. The prospect is always right—the prospect rules.

The objections may feel like a personal assault, and an attack—but they're not. Your first reaction will be to be defensive, to strike back. But instead, you probe some more, you ask questions, you begin getting deeper into the concern. You remain calm and poised, interested and understanding, confident, and positive.

Head up, shoulders back, spine straight. I find it helpful at this time to move a little closer to the prospect. As you listen, do so with great sensitivity and understanding. Seek out the important words. Listen for the emphasis. Observe. Tilt your body forward.

30 I consider objections the most important part of the entire process. They're not fun but if you do not probe for concerns, you will not know how effective your ask has been.

Is there anything that's keeping you from making a decision about your gift at this time?

That's a fairly good question that will help open up some other areas. A technique I have found to be extremely helpful is the *Feel, Felt, Found* response. It works in almost every situation.

You've done a good job, Jerry, but I've got to tell you that I'm still not sold. The tuition at the school is so darn high and you know I've got two kids there.

*I certainly know how you **feel**, John. I've got to tell you that I **felt** exactly the same way. When I took on this assignment, I began doing some probing. Let me tell you what I **found**. The tuition we're paying actually doesn't take care of the entire expense of educating our kids here at Park School. Do you know that our kids are being subsidized about $4,000 a year? That's the difference between what we pay and what it actually costs. I remind you that the purpose of this campaign is to raise money for an endowment that will help close the gap. I don't know about you, but I don't feel good about the school subsidizing my kids.*

Let me give you another example.

I'm interested in the project, Jerry, but I feel I give so much each year. You know, they never fail to come to me for a gift. I feel I pretty much do my share. If you want, I can give the same amount— but shift it from the annual giving to the capital program.

*When you talk about being stretched on the annual giving, John, I know exactly how you **feel**. I've been* *giving for a number of years, and I've* **felt** *exactly the same way when they first talked to me about getting involved in this program. I did some investigating and let me tell you what I* **found***. This kind of a capital program doesn't happen very often, and this one is so terribly important. This is something I just had to get involved in.*

It is terribly important, by the way, that you do nothing to cannibalize your annual giving. A person mustn't be allowed to transfer what they do annually to the capital program. You gain nothing. In fact, you lose—you lose the momentum and the ongoing rhythm of the annual giving.

31   As much as possible, try to anticipate what objections might be raised by the specific prospect you're calling on. Hopefully, you'll have enough history about this person that you can foresee what they might be. Address them early in your presentation in a positive way.

If the objection is weak, or not central to the issue, you may wish to ignore it. Not every concern has to be tackled. I find it helpful, if I am going to respond, to restate the objection—then answer it as clearly, as completely, and as quickly as possible.

If I understand you correctly, John, you feel . . .

Repeating the concern shows that it registered with you, you are empathetic, and that you really listened.

Never argue. You should tackle the objection, not beat down the person. Explain. Get more information if necessary. Avoid who is right. Keep stressing what is right.

Don't let the objections derail the presentation. You've done a wonderful job thus far! Handle objections as they come up. React positively, return to the main issue.

If possible, convert the objection into a reason for giving.

You've mentioned that you do not feel our faculty has been as strong as it has been in the past. That's precisely the reason we are raising these funds. We want to build an endowment sufficiently large so that we can . . .

Listen carefully. Do not ignore any major problem or issue.

In responding to an objection, use the four questions I refer to later in the book in detail.

- Is it the institution?
- Is it the project?
- Is it the amount I asked for?
- Is it the timing?

If you have the answer to these questions, you will know precisely the status of your gift.

I can't make a decision now, Jerry. I'm going to need some time to think it over.

Of course you are, John. A gift the size that we've been talking about is going to require some time to think about. But let me ask a question before I leave. It seems to me that as we talked, I had the feeling

*that you really cared greatly about the Boy Scouts—
that this group is really important to you.* **(Is it the
institution?)**

**You bet. I think the Scouts are one of the best or-
ganizations in the country. I went through the
whole thing myself and ended up an Eagle Scout.
I can tell you, they really changed my life.**

Great! I've passed the first hurdle. I know that my
prospect doesn't have a problem with the organization. Now on to the next question. I have to find out
how he feels about the project.

*Thanks, John. I was pretty certain you felt that way
about Scouting. But then let me just ask about the
project. I want to make certain I know how you feel
about it. I thought as we were talking, you were
really keen about the rebuilding program at the Boy
Scout Camp. You seemed particularly interested in
the new cabins.* **(Is it the project?)**

**Going to Boy Scout Camp was one of the greatest
experiences in my life. You bet the Camp interested me. And you guessed right. I was especially
interested in the cabins. The last time I visited
there, I thought they looked particularly seedy. I
am not certain that I would want to send a son of
mine to a camp and have them spend their time in
a cabin that looked like that.**

This couldn't be better. I have now discovered what I
thought to be the case—John is really interested in the
project. Best of all, I'm on target. He is interested in doing
something about a new cabin. That is what is of the greatest interest to him. So far so good.

Then, just let me ask you about the amount. When we talked about the program, we spoke about a gift of $50,000 to build a new cabin. I thought that's about the amount that you would want to give. Isn't that right, isn't that about what you would want to give?

Note how I phrase the question. I didn't say that $50,000 was the amount that I had asked for, or the amount that we had him down for—horrors! But rather, I say that this is the amount that we felt certain that he would want to give.

Well, the truth is, Jerry, it's a little bit more than I had thought about but—yeah, that's about what I would like to do.

I'm close, I'm really close. This is one of the great experiences of life. As mystically close as being in on creation! I feel certain now that I am going to get the gift. There's only one more hurdle. It must be the timing that is bothering John.

I'm so pleased to hear that. I was pretty certain that was about the amount that you would want to give. And the cabin you've been talking about (Now I am assuming that the gift is going to be made, and that's the kind of positive-reinforcement you ought to indicate at this point in the solicitation.) *is going to be so important. There will be hundreds and hundreds of scouters through the years who will benefit by what you have done. And you'll have the satisfaction of knowing that you made it possible.* (Win-win.) *I've got to ask—is it the timing of the gift that is a problem?* (**Is it the timing?**) *Would you like a little bit more time than the three years we talked about in order to make the gift of $50,000?* (I'm providing more time, but I am reinforcing the $50,000.)

Well, I still haven't said I am going to do it. But if I had a little extra time, I think I could swing it. Let's say I had five years. I think I could do it in that time. But I still need some time to think about it.

Praise be to God. I think I have the gift. I'm singing hymns. I hear a flourish of trumpets.

32   You've come to the end of your ask. (You're doing wonderfully.) Now you must make certain that you get a commitment to something. It's obvious on the call I just wrote about that I am not going to get the gift on this visit. It very seldom happens on the first call. In fact, if it does—chances are you haven't gotten the gift at a high enough level.

But I can't leave the visit without a commitment to something. We have to set a time for another visit. If we don't get a date right then, it may never be done. You know how tough it was getting the first visit.

That's great, John, and I do want to give you time to think this over. Get out your calendar, and let's set a time for another visit.

Oh, we don't have to do that now. I'll give you a call and we can set a time—or I'll just call and let you know about my decision.

We both seem so frantically busy and you remember how difficult it was to get together for this visit. Let's set a date now. I'll just get out my calendar, too. And I would prefer seeing you in person than trying to handle this on the telephone. It's that important, and your involvement means so much to us.

33   One thing I've finally discovered is that the opposite
     of interest isn't disinterest. It's apathy.

     I suspect that you have had the same experience as I
     in talking to a prospect. You're doing your very best,
     you're as eloquent as you can possibly be, you're
     making your eleven minutes as magical as possi-
     ble—and the prospect's expression is as blank as a
     waiter's stare. You're in trouble. You need to shake
     things up somehow, do some serious probing, ask
     some questions that will unlock this ice jam.

     Here's a question you ought to ask. Frame it in a way
     that sounds most like you. But make these words
     work. Note, also, that it's an open question that can't
     be answered *yes* or *no*. The prospect has to *give* you
     an answer.

     *Tell me a little bit how you feel about what we have
     discussed.*

34   Those who are the most effective in getting the gift,
     both volunteers and professionals, believe heart and
     soul in their organization. They are dedicated and
     committed completely and fully. They are confident,
     also, in the value that they add as solicitors. They
     have loyalty, pride, and devotion for the organization
     and their donors and prospects. It comes through in
     everything they say and do. Their enthusiasm is in-
     fectious. One thing we know: If there is any lack of
     ardor or zeal, it shows. You need what Dr. Samuel
     Johnson referred to as men (and women), "so inspir-
     ited with ardor, and so fortified with resolution, that
     they persevere and are successful."

FasTrack tenets

"No, Jerry—Thursday's out! How about never—is never good for you?"

1   Reasons you didn't get the gift:

    • Inadequate preparation.

    • Anxiety.

- You assume too much.

- Failure to probe.

- Poor listening.

- Too much emphasis on features, and not enough on benefits.

- Premature selling.

- You did not make it a win-win situation.

2   Use the **FLAG** system for determining who in your database has the greatest potential for making a major gift:

> **F**requency of the gifts
>
> **L**ength of giving
>
> **A**ffinity for the organization
>
> **G**iving size

3   In asking for a gift:

- Begin by knowing everything possible about the institution, its program, and the project.

- Find out everything you can about the donor and his or her giving history.

- After a careful analysis, determine the amount you should ask for.

- Give some thought as to how you will express the amount of your request. Say it out loud several times before your visit.

- Eighty-five percent of getting the gift is setting up the time for your visit. Keep in mind that your job is to set the date for the visit—not to make the case and not to get the gift on the telephone.

- Practice, practice, practice.

- Write out in advance all of the reasons you might be given for objecting to a visit. Learn how to respond.

- Call in pairs and go to your best prospects first.

- During the visit, use your early moments to establish a rapport and common ground. Take as much time as necessary to create the proper environment—but remember your objective is to talk about the project and get the gift.

- It is essential that you probe for concerns. Use open questions.

- Conversation gives you the opportunity to listen.

- Take no more than 11 minutes to present the project and its rationale.

- The case for the project has to be relevant, have dramatic and emotional appeal, and provide a sense of urgency.

- You must convey the benefit to the donor.

- Do not let the size of the gift dominate the presentation.

- Don't sell features. Talk about outcomes.

- One of the most important elements of the presentation is to give testimony to your own gift and what others have done.

- When finally making the ask, use words such as: "I would like you to consider a gift of . . ."

- Don't get rattled by objections. They are your best friends. You must probe for concerns. If you don't, you will not know how the prospect really feels about the program.

- You must get a commitment to something before leaving—either the gift or the date for another visit.

4

You Can't Be A Winner If You Don't Get In The Race

Get ready. When you complete this chapter, you will know everything that is important about asking for a gift, a fail-proof process that ensures your success. But it won't be necessarily easy.

A fundraiser stood at the heavenly gate.
His face was scarred and old.
He stood before the man of fate
For admission to the fold.

"What have you done," Saint Peter said,
"To gain admission here?"
"I've been a fundraiser, sir," he said,
"For many and many a year."

The pearly gate swung open wide,
Saint Peter rang the bell.
"Come in and choose your harp," he sighed,
"You've had your share of hell!"

For me, one of the great satisfactions I have is asking men and women to invest in great causes, towering dreams, and everlasting benefits to those who are served. For me, every moment with a potential donor is a spiritual adventure, scourging excitement mixed with a mighty mission. What other profession in life provides such peak opportunities?

The really difficult part in fundraising is not in getting people to give money. That's easy. The tough part is asking. That's often true of volunteers, and the sad truth is that many of our professional fund raisers don't like to ask for money either. Professionals who feel trepidation inspire very little confidence in the trembling hearts of their volunteers.

Note this well: Asking for a gift is not selling, it's not razzle-dazzle. It's partly repetition, and partly just doing the right things. That, and having antennae that vibrate with the right instincts. I'm a great believer in instinct. I feel that a person with intuition that pulsates does all of the internal data-gathering and processing, evaluates unconsciously all the *stuff* for the subconscious to chew on. The reflexes are swift and the results without error.

I love it. For me, making the call is not the destination—it's the journey. The fun is in the doing. You place your faith in visions, ideas, wonderful people, and the nobility of a great cause. Add to that a little bit of genius and great deal of plod.

I've been at it a long time, but I still don't consider myself an expert on the subject. I am reminded that the Titanic was built by experts and Noah's ark by a rank amateur. And I certainly don't get a gift at the level I seek with every call I make. Michael Jordan likes to say that in his career, he has missed nearly ten thousand shots, lost over three thousand games, and there were times he took the decisive shot at the end of the game and missed at least fifty. "I have failed over and over in my life . . . and that is why I succeed."

There are times I don't get the gift I had hoped for. When that happens, I seldom feel that it is my failure—perhaps in not saying the right words or misplaced timing. It's seldom techniques. Techniques will, I believe, actually defeat the gift. Dr. Robert Schuller says: "It's never a problem with the way a program is presented and it isn't a problem with techniques—it's almost always an idea problem." Your program does indeed have to have a certain magic, a sense of urgency, a relevance that is impregnable.

Before and after every ask, I go through a period of intense introspection—always examining, and dissecting what happened, and exploring new ways I might consider for doing things. Every call, in a sense, is a homecoming—a journey by strength, determination, and planning.

I encourage you to find your own words, your own rhythm. They say that Miles Davis created great music by opening the space between the notes and stepping inside. If you find you own rhythm, you will find your soul.

I am never totally satisfied with my achievement or completely pleased with the results. I always feel that I could have done better. I take some comfort in what Aristotle tells us: "At the Olympic Games, it is not the finest and the strongest who are really crowned, but all those who entered the race." I covet for you the great joy of entering the race. I find great satisfaction even when the gift isn't as large as I hoped, and that does happen at times. I take some solace in knowing that half a loaf is still bread!

I'll give you the **7 Ps** of getting the gift. This is no philosophical whirling dervish, like the Wizard of Oz with all the gadgets working.

The **7 Ps** are the basics, the fundamentals. Actually, everything you need to know about securing the gift is covered. Just follow the basics. It's much like what Michelangelo said: "It's simple. Just hammer off everything that doesn't belong on the sculpture."

1　**Prepare.**　Before you make the contact, be completely prepared. Know everything there is to know about the prospect, everything you can get your hands on. If there is some giving history to the institution, analyze that.

Determine in advance a general idea of the amount you should ask for. It's all right to think in ranges at this point (a $100,000 to $150,000 gift, for instance) but remember when you actually ask for the gift, you suggest a specific amount.

If possible, know what the donor has given to other programs and institutions. Get as much inside of the person's head as possible. And know just as much information about the spouse. Determine if there is unlimited juice in that orange. It will help you set the figure for your ask.

If there is no history of giving, it will be tough. The first gift is the most difficult. It's a case of the-first-olive-out-of-the-jar-is-the-most-difficult. Find out who among your institution's family may know the person well enough to open the door or join you in the visit. In our business, we know that everything is connected to everything. It's what Somerset Maugham called: *the long arm of coincidence.*

2 **Practice.** In everything you do, practice your comments and responses. Develop the scenario of what you feel will happen. I find it helpful to make a written outline. Practice! Practice! Practice!

Don't worry if the actual call turns out to be different than what you scripted. It most often is. Isn't this what makes our work so challenging—and so much fun? Practice is important because it ratchets up the courage. It helps prepare you for virtually any contingency. "Sometimes," the great film director Fellini said, "if you pull a little tail, you will find an elephant at the other end." You are never certain what you will find when you get into your call. That's part of the great joy and exhilaration of this business. Emotions come thick and fast.

3 **Poise.** We find in our research that one of the major factors in not getting a gift is that the solicitor revealed an uneasiness and anxiety that flawed the presentation. Being poised means understanding the dignity and worth of fulfilled challenging expectations. You represent a great cause. Because of your work, countless will benefit. Because of what you do, lives will be changed and saved.

You need never apologize. Screw-up your courage. You are bound to get tough questions and serious objections. Count on it. If you don't, chances are you haven't probed sufficiently to get the gift. Get your confidence to a level that you understand that when a prospect slams a door in your face—it will only be to keep you from leaving! Remember, each question and each objection is the next important step to securing the gift. The prospect is helping you understand what will help give comfort and confidence to his or her areas of doubt.

Here's where your poise will show. Take the objection as a reward and bonus the prospect has given you. It's a present. It's the necessary step in leading you to the gift. Feel much like the wife of New York Mayor Hyland's wife who said to Queen Marie of Romania, when her majesty visited in the early 1920s: "Queen, you said a mouthful."

Answer the concerns with directness, without ambiguity, and with proper sensitivity and understanding on your part. You need to show that the inquiry or objection is a true concern of substantial value. That's why you are taking the proper time to respond unhurriedly and with empathy. You are now much closer to getting the gift.

4   **Positive.**   I will ask you to bear with me on this. Some will think it mumbo-jumbo. But I believe it with all my heart and soul, and I practice it every opportunity I have. I call it my *Attitude Audition*. It is the ability to mentally prepare for a meeting or a presentation and to conjure up very positive results, optimistic and exuberant, and in specific terms.

I rivet my thoughts to the visit. I think about how effective I shall be. My radar is totally focused on my ask and how clear and compelling it will be. I think it, I visualize it, I get it. I know how that sounds, but I really believe that it works.

Dr. Abraham Maslow describes it as self-actualization—the phenomenon in people to make real his or her full potential, to be everything that he or she can be. Each time you make the contact and the call, I want you to visualize in advance the entire session and how well it is going to go. Think about the results. Go ahead. Try it.

I learned my lesson at the feet of the master. I was talking with W. Clement Stone, the great advocate of *Positive Mental Attitude*. He told me how he consciously trained his mind to reject negative suggestions. He told me: "If someone tells me that it can't be done or you're not going to be able to do that—my subconscious mind instantly shoots a message to my conscious mind—*maybe he can't . . . but I can.*"

Where a negative person sees problems, a person with a positive mental attitude sees only opportunities. That's what visualization and a positive attitude will do for you.

Benjamin Zander, a conductor at the Boston Philharmonic, says: "I set as my ultimate objective what I believe my full capacity is—and I settle for nothing less. I think about it, I visualize it. I have an unsinkable positive attitude. I make myself a relentless architect of the possibilities that exist." It is consistent among the peak performers I have worked with—this virtual unshakable belief in the certainty of their own success. They are positive, not cocky—but totally success/ordered. They have interminable self-confidence.

A positive attitude. That's it. Visualizing and knowing that you can do it. It is an unshakable faith that time will prove you right. You understand that any situation that may seem like a defeat is merely minor and temporary. You have the ability to focus on the next opportunity and the conviction that the next time, you will be successful. You are starting over, but with even greater confidence, spirit, and exuberance.

In the studies I have done, my peak performers report a highly developed ability to imprint images of successful actions in their mind. They write the script and rehearse it. They practice mentally those specific skills and behaviors and achievements that lead to outcomes and achievements that they ultimately attain.

5   **Persuasive.** I don't find it surprising that some of the very most effective fundraisers I know, both professionals and volunteers, aren't the men and women you would normally select for the role from central casting. The ones I consider to be truly great seem to come in all sizes and shapes, all ages, and of course, both men and women. *I often find that the best man for the job is a woman.*

These great fundraisers, these skilled askers, are not brazen, brassy barkers. You know the kind I mean. Loud, back-slapping and the kind of person who in a fifty-fifty deal even keeps the hyphen. It takes someone who is quietly and confidently persuasive. It requires a case that is relevant, emotionally and dramatically appealing, and with a high sense of resolve and urgency. Relevant, dramatic, and urgent— says it all. There's that special moment in the presentation when vision and urgency become poetry.

You can't push or press the prospect. It may take more time than you like. It often does. But you must keep soldiering toward your objective—getting the gift.

The great French Marshal Lyautey once asked his gardener to plant a tree. The gardener objected that the tree the Marshal wanted was a slow-growing variety that would not reach maturity for a hundred years. The Marshal replied: "In that case, there's no time to lose. Plant it immediately."

If there is no sense of urgency, there is no reason for the donor to make that gift now. They have to understand what the consequences are if the gift is not made. *If we do not have the funds now, we shall not be able to move forward. . . .* Or *four hundred youngsters a day will die in this country if we don't have the funds now to. . . .* You get the idea.

Success is ensured when there is a sense of urgency, a demand for excellence, and a persistent discontent with the way things are. Donors are persuaded and prone to what I call the *tyranny of the urgent.*

We were about to begin work at a small college in Ohio when we found out the Vice President was to be fired. (It does happen.) I asked why. The President told me that Frank had redefined the concept of *mañana.* "His version is like mañana as in Mexico, but without the same sense of urgency."

There needs to be a healthy impatience that is threaded through the fabric of the presentation and proposal. You will not achieve your objective without it. It is one of the most important and telling factors of success. It is your most telling directional sign on the road to persuading your prospect. If you impart the urgency, you win.

When Shakespeare's Glendower boasts that "I can call spirits from the vastly deep"—Hotspur brings him down to size with this answer. "Why, so can I, and so can anyone. But will they come when you do call them?" Shakespeare gives us a lesson. Only those who are persuasive, the noblest and brightest, will receive a proper response.

To be persuasive, the fundraiser must weave an appropriate spell and provide an effective message—all within something comparable to the gossamer-spinning and webcasting spider. Seek the prowess of the spider. You want a combination of what Thomas Hoving, former President of the Metropolitan Museum of Art, called *flare, outcry, and passion.*

Tom Peters says: "Passion for the cause doesn't guarantee success. On the other hand, a lack of passion does ensure failure." In making the ask, we must *become chariots of fire*, for which the best word is exultation. It will happen. I suggest you commit deeply to your own instincts regarding the project, enter an adventure zone where doors of possibility and fulfillment open—and something seemingly miraculous happens. As Red Buttons used to say: "Strange things are happening."

6   **Persistence.** William Barrett writes in *The Illusion of Technique* about the runner who is lapped by the entire field of other runners. He staggers, he stumbles, he keeps torturing himself to keep going. Bar-

rett describes this as more admirable than the victory of the winner we crown. Persistence, perseverance—that wins the gift.

Hardly a day goes by that fundraisers do not meet defeat of some kind or sort. We feel some sense of failure, disappointment, and distress. "Life is fired at you point-blank," writes Ortega. That's when a high level of determination has to kick in.

I am convinced that you can do anything you wish in fundraising, and be as successful as you desire—if you are willing to understand that a *no* doesn't always mean *no*—and do whatever is necessary to overcome the objection and to persevere. The only failure is when you don't try.

The gift is made because someone with conviction makes a greater effort and never gives up. You can be successful if you are determined. Joe Frazier likens himself to the Baby Huey inflatable doll: "I'm big, I'm ugly, but when you knock me down, I come right back at you."

You persevere. You understand that if you want the rainbow you have to put up with the rain. We face them all the time, prospects who are stubborn and difficult to budge, seemingly implacable and immovable. I am convinced that you can overcome this if you have the faith, the desire, and the willingness to sustain the struggle. The difference between the successful fundraiser and the one who is not—is not due to a lack of knowledge or ability, but rather a lack of dogged determination and commitment, head, and heart.

> *Persistence prevails,*
> *When all else fails.*

7   **Patience.** At times in this business, we all walk a tight rope. We want the gift, because we know how much it will mean to the institution and all who are served. We want it, too, because we know what great joy it will bring to the donor.

We understand full well that a gift cannot be made without it somehow coming back to the donor. The old Jewish expression is indeed true: The more you give, the more you get back. We know that through giving, donors get within themselves, attain a height never before known, and get to know their true selves.

"I want to know myself," Socrates told Phaedrus. The donor becomes sanctified, and is incapable of cynicism and negativism. They feel the exhilaration of being able to change lives and save lives. But somehow, they also sense that greatness lies in being able to not only remake the organization but in being able to remake themselves. They can stumble into the future but they have decided instead to create their own destiny for others. Donors don't sit on the sidelines watching the game of life. They choose to get into the fray.

There comes a time when no matter how carefully you prepare and practice, and no matter how persuasive and golden your words, the prospect seems immovable. There are some you call on who sadly keep you mindful that no matter how hard you try, you can't milk a bull. It's not productive, and the bull doesn't like it.

I've had those days myself. Plenty. Even my fortune cookie once read: *Your request for no MSG was ignored.*

If I feel there is any hope at all, I will not give in. I will carefully calculate how many more contacts I should make before giving up. I won't hang on forever—there are too many other good prospects to call on. But if there is hope, I shall prevail. I shall pursue my prospect with ardor and patient-aggressiveness.

I understand full well that no matter how difficult and stressful some prospects are, if there is any hope at all for a gift—no matter how great the assault on spirit and soul, I shall survive and thrive. I have found that if you are outcome-oriented, you must be patient. It is the yeast and patient-fermentation that does the job. I understand that patience helps me stay in the game and ride it wherever and whenever it will go, calling its own rhythms and promises.

Alexander Wollcott said to his fellow alumni at Hamilton College: "Some of you are successes and some are failures. And only God knows which are which." I have found that getting a *no* certainly does not make you a failure. A *no* very often means only *not now.*

I try to have the agility and flexibility to change course, to solve a problem creatively, to deal immediately with challenges, and try to determine most effectively how I can meet the needs of the donor. I realize that patience will help me understand that a delay may not necessarily mean the prospect was negative about the project or disenchanted with my presentation. It's very often the case that I have not made it clear to the donor how he or she will benefit. I try my **5 As—Anticipate, Adapt, Adopt, Adjust**, and **Achieve**. And I am convinced that I shall achieve. I try to combine the creativity of a genius with the patience of a poker player.

Follow these **7 Ps.** Your calls will be filled with success. That's a promise. Your contacts will overflow with drama and excitement. There will, of course, be disappointments along the way. As Molière said: "Life is a play with a badly written Third Act."

There are really no formulas, no proud answers. I do know that you can't be a winner if you don't get in the race. I know that commitment and motivation are more important than techniques and razzle-dazzle. I am convinced that if it is not fun, you probably won't succeed. I know that if you are not committed to the project and the institution, you will never feel fulfilled. Most of all, I know that the gift has to help the prospect fulfill his or her needs. If you can achieve all of that, you have the gift. You will be as Franz Kafka observed, "The ax that breaks the frozen sea within."

I want to set the record straight. You've heard the pundit: "Keep calling. It's a game of numbers. If you make enough calls, you will get appointments. If you get enough appointments, you will get a gift. You can't miss." Very plausible, but very wrong! It's one of the old truisms—that isn't true. Keep calling, that's certainly facing in the right direction. But mind you, it's not a game of making enough calls. The reward goes to those who make *quality* calls.

Quality and persistence will win the day. The great Prime Minister of England, Benjamin Disraeli, said: "After the final *no* there comes a *yes*. And on that *yes*, the future well depends. *No* was the night. *Yes* is the present sun." Persistence will provide the light in your quest.

FASTRACK TENETS

Practice the **7 Ps** for getting the gift.

> **Prepare** as completely as possible for the visit. Understand everything you can about the institution and the donor.

> **Practice** your comments and responses. Make a written outline. And make certain you list all of the possible reasons a person might object, and have a response for them.

> **Poise** helps you overcome objections and provides assurance.

> **Positive** mental attitude puts you in the right frame of mind. It allows you to visualize the possibilities and assure success.

> **Persuasive** interpretation is important, but not the *loud and back-slapping* variety. It comes from having a passion for the organization and the project—and passion is the most important factor in gaining the gift.

> **Persistence** is one of the most important elements in getting the gift. The donor very seldom moves at your speed. It takes time. And that means perseverance.

> **Patience** is a component of the process that we must live with. Practice what Shakespeare wrote on the subject:

> Patience is a virtue—
> From that you must not drift.
> It's the only way certain,
> That you will get the gift.

(Okay, okay—so Shakespeare didn't write it. You get the idea anyway!)

In asking for a gift, you must engage the **Five As**

Anticipate
Adapt
Adopt
Adjust
Achieve

5

The Four Magic Questions

If I must say so myself, I thought I had made quite a good presentation of the case and the project. Perhaps short of brilliant—but not bad at all.

I had listened carefully, probed when necessary for more information, searched for areas of interest, and maintained intent eye contact. We had come to that charged moment—frightening (I'll refer to that later) and awesome, when the air is ablaze with hope and high expectation. The time had come . . . I was about to ask Dick for his gift.

I had rehearsed well. I paraphrase Churchill's admonition into fundraising terms, and I coach others and try to practice it myself: *There is nothing as effective and successful as a very well rehearsed, carefully scripted, spontaneous ask!*

The visit had gone pretty much as planned. But do you often feel as I do? No matter how often I have asked for a gift, I still have haunting thoughts that race through my mind before I speak those magic words that hopefully will produce the gift: Did I probe enough? Do I really know Dick's primary interest? Did I ask enough questions? Did I talk enough about the great benefits and how his gift would change lives? Did I get Dick to talk enough? Am I asking for the right amount?

Wait . . . perhaps I should plan for another visit. Is the time precisely right? I could come back another time.

I decide to ask. Of course!

I follow my own preaching: It is better to make the ask, even if all factors do not fit my perfect blueprint, then not to make the ask at all. Better: Ready, Fire, Aim . . . than Ready, Aim, Aim, Aim . . .

I use the words that I find most comfortable for making the ask—or if you prefer, *presenting the opportunity.*

"Dick . . . I would like you to consider a gift of $100,000. Your involvement will save lives for a generation to come and transform this into one of the great cardiac centers of the country." The words, *I would like you to consider* are what I find most appropriate for setting-up the request.

Ah, I have now asked Dick for his gift. That wasn't so difficult after all.

PAUSE

(I follow the example I teach others. Make the ask and stop. Don't fill in the silence. No matter how long it may seem—wait. Follow the admonition: The first one

who speaks is dead! And so I pause . . . for what seems
eternity. Dick finally responds.)

**No, I don't think so. I don't think I can give
that much, not at this time.**

And now, kind reader, you have been with me this
far. You've probably been in the same situation. I heard
one of four responses I could have received. Which of the
four is it? Is it a *Yes* . . . a *Maybe* on its way to a *Yes* . . . a
Maybe on its way to a *No* . . . or a *No*.

You're perhaps thinking in Dick's case, it's a *Maybe*
on its way to a *No*. Or a *No*. You gather your things, thank
Dick for the visit and his time, you leave the proposal behind and ask that he consider it.

Wrong!

You have come only to the beginning of your ask.
There is still important work and delving to be done. Your
task now begins. Join me for the remainder of this presentation. It really happened and Dick is alive and a wonderfully generous person. In this case, it followed the
script. It doesn't always.

To my way of thinking, the response was actually a
Maybe on its way to a *Yes*. How many of you guessed the
same? If you did, you would have done precisely what I
did next. I probed.

Here's what gave me the courage and encouragement to move forward. Keep in mind that *No* doesn't always mean *no*—sometimes it means *yes* . . . *but I need
some more time to think it over . . . or . . . not now, but*

maybe later . . . or . . . I really need to talk this over with some other folks—my spouse, my accountant, or whomever.

It's time for you to seek, search, and study. There are only four puzzles that you have to unlock. The key is waiting for your careful questioning.

There are four riddles you have to find the answer to. To my way of thinking, there aren't three and there aren't five. I'll put these in the form of questions. I always ask them in this sort of a situation: A *Maybe* on its way to a *Yes*, or a *Maybe* on its way to a *No*. If I don't ask these four questions, I'll leave and never know where we stand with the donor. And if I return for a subsequent visit, I still won't have the information I need to move forward with a successful ask.

I must find out how Dick really feels, I am going to review my four questions now and in a subsequent chapter. Repetition is enlightening and good for your soul! And the concept is that important. I must find out whether Dick's response is a *Maybe* because:

1   There is not a great feeling or involvement with the *institution*. Is there a certain lack of passion and identification with its mission and vision?

2   There is a lack of interest in the specific *project*. Is this a program for which the donor has neither heart nor spirit?

3   Was it the *amount*? Did I ask for too much? Was this beyond anything the donor might have had in mind?

4   The *timing* is a factor. Would the donor be more willing to give if the timing was changed, extended, put off for a year?

I must know the answer to these immutable questions: Is it the organization . . . the project . . . the amount . . . or the timing? I mustn't leave a *Maybe* until I know the answer to these questions. (This is true of even a *No*. But more about that later.) If I don't find out, I won't know what to do next, and I'll never get the gift.

I'll tell you in a moment what happened regarding the remainder of my visit with Dick. You might guess that I was successful. That's because consultants have a tendency never to talk about those contacts they make that are unsuccessful—although the truth of it is . . . there are more of the latter than the former. (But why admit to that sort of thing when you hope that others will perceive you as invincible?)

Now I'll stop for a moment for a small interruption. I promise it will be instructive. Note it well. We teach a form of prospect and donor management that is fail-proof. You simply cannot miss. Many call it *Moves Management*©. That's how it is best known. But no matter what it is called, it ensures your success. I referred to it in an earlier chapter.

If you have a prospect management system that is in place, and you are working the program—you will know the answers to the four intractable questions before you ever ask for the gift. That is the great joy and secret to the success of a prospect management system.

But if you're in the same situation that I'm mostly involved in, or in an intensive and short-term campaign, and these are my life—you don't have the luxury of multi-visits over an extended period. Two or three visits, bang. You may have to be satisfied with that. This is when I want you to employ the four questions I've indicated. They're magic.

Back to Dick and the remainder of my visit. I had made my first request. But as we both agreed (if you've been paying attention), that is often just the beginning. Or as Churchill said: ". . . the end of the beginning." Dick made his response, which to some may have seemed negative—but you and I know better. I couldn't leave without probing further, not if I wanted the gift. Here's how the rest of the visit went. There isn't space to give you all of the detail, but you know well enough to fill in much of the back and forth.

> *Dick, thanks for responding so clearly to my re-quest.* (Ah, but we know it wasn't really clear and certainly not final.) *And I did hear what you said. I don't mean to press you on the matter . . . but I feel I must ask you a question. Do bear with me. Is there something that bothers you about the hospital?* (**Is it the institution?**) *You have been a supporter for so long and you have done so much in the past, I was quite certain that you feel very positive about our present work and our vision for the future. Do you still feel that same warmth, friendship, and support?*
>
> **Oh, yes. Now, probably more than ever. I think they're doing a great job, more impor-tant than ever.** (I'm past the first hurdle.)
>
> *I was pretty certain that was the way you felt. But I also sensed that this was the kind of proj-ect that would really interest you—that the new*

Cardiac Center had real meaning for you. Particularly because of your own situation and your family experience with heart problems. Is there something about the project that causes you to hesitate? (**Is it the project?**)

Oh, no. Certainly not. On the contrary, the Center is something I feel is tremendously important, something we should have at the hospital.

(Great! We can now cross out that question. But more than that, Dick said *we*. I call that: a "Gotcha!" And now to the tough question. If we get by this one, we have the gift.)

Well tell me then, Dick, did I ask for too much? I need to know. I honestly felt that based on your close identification with the hospital and your past generous support, $100,000 was just about the amount that you would want to give to a program that is this important. Am I correct? That is about the amount you would want to give, isn't it?

(For the past dozen years or so, Dick has been making an annual gift to the hospital of between $5,000 and $10,000. There were a couple of years that he missed for some reason, but other than that, he's been fairly consistent. The $100,000 request is certainly reasonable, following my rule that the request for a major capital venture can be somewhere between ten and twenty-five times the regular annual giving. I felt I wouldn't be far off with this request to Dick of $100,000. Note, also, that I didn't say anything such as: *This is the amount that we hoped you would give.* Instead, I used the term: *This is the amount that we thought you would want to give.*)

This was working out better than I could have hoped. Still, remember my questions—they are unalterable. (Remember Question #3: **Is it the amount**?)

Dick responds: **No, you were correct—that's just about the amount that I would like to give to a project like this.** (Yea! In my mind, I'm doing a high-five.)

And now, my final question.

Is it the timing, then, Dick. Is it the timing that's off? You've already indicated your enthusiasm and excitement for the Cardiac Center. And you told me that the amount was what you would want to give. Is the timing a problem? Would you like more time to make a gift like this? Maybe an extra year or two?

That's it exactly, said Dick. And then he went on to tell me it would be impossible to make a gift, even a small one, at this time. He was so heavily committed to a couple other projects that there simply weren't funds available.

I responded as you would expect. *But that's the easiest part of all, Dick. Don't worry a bit about the timing. We can easily work that out. The important thing is that you are included in this important program and that you are able to do what you hoped. Let's extend the timing. Do you feel that you could make your first payment in a year or so, or do you need more time than that?*

When you make your payment is not as impor-
tant as having you a part of the project. This
new Cardiac Center has to have your involve-
ment. It will be easy to work out the timing.

From that point, it was great fun. Dick felt that he could make a small payment a year from now, and then make equal payments the next three years to fulfill his commitment. He was absolutely delighted. And everyone won. Dick was able to do what he really wanted to do, I was in a position to help make it happen, and the hospital is one step closer toward its new Cardiac Center. Everyone wins.

That's the story about Dick. Now, I want to talk about the three other responses and what they mean. Should you feel good about a *Yes*—and how can you tell? Perhaps the gift should have been for more. As you likely guessed, I'm going to tell you that a *No* is not the end. It's not even the beginning of the end. It's almost certainly only the end of the beginning. And how about a *Maybe* on its way to a *No*? Can this be turned around?

My four probing inquiries, however, will get you through all situations. They must be used. Go ahead, make note of them now: **Is it the institution, the project, the amount, or the timing?** You mustn't leave the visit without finding the answers to these questions.

And now, something I refer to much earlier in this chapter. Well . . . let's have a moment of truth. I have been *shaking the tambourine*, as they say, for a long time. I have made a kazillion asks, and have my share, perhaps more than my share, of success.

But I never fail to have the same sense of excitement, awe, trepidation, and challenge—each time I ask someone to invest in a program. Some say that this is good, that when you lose that bundle of flying butterflies in the tummy, you lose your effectiveness. That may be true, but I wish I was beyond that. I must tell you that I always feel about the same: My hands get moist and there's perspiration on my upper lip. My throat gets very dry, and my tongue gets thick. And there seems to be a chicken bone stuck in my throat.

Where, oh where, is that wondrous flow of dazzling words that I so carefully rehearsed? If you feel the same, don't worry. We all do. And I assure you: The more often you make an ask, the easier it does become. It really does.

So, for those who have some concern—take heart. We're in this together. We all feel the same—and I've probably been working at this longer than you. You may feel like the poet Stevie Smith who wrote: "I was much further out in the water than you thought. And I wasn't waving. I was drowning."

But you will be successful, more often than not. That's a promise. You represent a worthy organization and a great cause. And keep in mind: If you're in a forest hunting, and you just sit at a clearing long enough— sooner or later, a deer will cross your path.

Here's the answer: rehearse, rehearse, rehearse. Probe as much as you can. Get the prospect to speak. Listen. Be certain you ask my unalterable questions. You'll get the gift.

See. It wasn't as tough as you thought You'll be so eager to practice your new-found skills, you'll be stopping people on the street to ask for a gift. In the next chapter, I'll complete the rest of my sermon.

FasTrack Tenets

In making an ask, you must find out from the prospect:

1   What their attitude is about the institution, how much identification and passion do they have for it.

2   How much interest do they have in the specific project.

3   Did you ask for the proper amount.

4   Is the timing right for the gift.

If you don't know the answers to these questions, you will not understand the prospect's true feeling regarding making a gift. Probe, examine, ask questions—make certain you know the answers to these questions.

"That's truly an impressive finish to your presentation, Jerry—but I still don't believe I'd be interested in making a gift to the University."

6

You'll Get The Gift

I was having dinner recently with Stanley Marcus. He's the genius and inspiration who built Neiman Marcus into one of the world's most successful merchandising enterprises. He is the patron and cheerleader of all good things that have happened in Dallas in the last fifty years.

He told me that he had just taken on the chairmanship of the Dallas Symphony's 75th Anniversary, $75 million campaign. "Stanley, you've done it all," I said. "You've headed every major effort in Dallas and the State, and plenty around the country. You're in your eighties now. (Late eighties, as a matter of fact.) Why would you take on something like this?"

"Two reasons," he said. "I love the Symphony. That's the first reason. And the most important reason is that I'm still paying back what I owe this community."

I reminded him that he is considered one of the nation's greatest marketing and sales shamans of this last half century. "There must be times," I asked, "when you get a *no* for an answer when you ask for a gift. How does it make you feel when you get turned down?"

Without a moment's pause, he said: "I never take *no* for an answer. Even if the person dies, I consider it only a *maybe!*"

That's what Samuel Taylor Coleridge refers to as "the willing suspension of disbelief." Unlike anyone I have ever met, Stanley Marcus exhibits the magic of the conceivable. He says that to accept something as impossible is completely unacceptable. That's Marcus' attitude. I'd like to see more of this do-something, positive attitude demonstrated by all of us who are involved in the business of asking others to invest in our causes. An undisciplined optimism for the fray and venture, that's what I'd like to see.

And now, kind reader, to continue the sermon. If you remember, I admonished you to ask the four unalterable questions to a response of a *maybe* or a *no* to your request for a gift. You need to determine if the lack of enthusiasm and affirmation is because of:

1 The Institution

2 The project

3 The amount you asked for

4 The timing

The probing of these questions, or, as William Faulkner put it, "The seeking of eternal truths and verities," is certain to lead you to success. You'll need to know the answer before proceeding with your request.

I mentioned in the last chapter how Dick's *maybe* lead to a $100,000 gift because of the kind of probing I suggested. In this case, it was a *maybe* on its way to a *yes*.

We need not spend too much time on the *yes*—other than to say beware that you may have settled for too little.

Ask For Enough

Let me set the stage. You made the presentation and if you must say so, it was quite eloquent! There was drama and emotional appeal, and a sense of urgency. You asked for a specific amount. (Remember: do not give a range. The amount must be specific.) The emotions come thick and fast. The donor says *yes* to your request. You got the gift. It is one of the high experiences of life—as mystically close as being in on creation.

But wait. You may not actually have been as successful as you think. You may not have asked for enough.

If you have been using a donor and prospect management system, you'll have a good idea of precisely how much to ask for. The answer becomes quite clear if you make enough significant contacts. The operative word here is: significant.

But it doesn't always work out that way. Let me tell you about Tommy. In this particular situation, I had only one opportunity to make an ask. There are a lot of reasons I had to ask for the gift on this first visit, but it certainly isn't the best procedure and I don't recommend it. Worse still, in this case—we had absolutely no idea what Tommy would give. We were fairly sure that it ought to be in the range of one million dollars. He had been giving

$50,000 a year for the past four or five years. At that level, it would be right in the range of a million dollars (ten to twenty-five times annual giving).

Let's set the stage.

We're in a corner of Tommy's office, he on the couch and I in the chair next to him. His secretary brings us coffee. We sit and talk for about an hour. The bonding between us is very strong, even though this is the first time we have met. There is something very special about Tommy, and it would be difficult not to like him immensely. The chemistry is good, and we both can feel it. You've had that feeling yourself, right? When you just know you've clicked with someone.

We chat for the first twenty or thirty minutes—establishing what we call in our seminars, "Rapport and common ground." This is nothing special. You all do it, and probably very effectively.

I make the case for a small Methodist college. I thought I did so with cogency and grace. There are times that you are *good*, and times you are *less than good*. On this visit, I was *good!*

We come to that moment. I say: "Tommy, it is quite clear to me how enthusiastic you are about the College, and how excited you are about this particular program. I would like you to consider a gift of one million dollars." (*"I would like you consider"* being the magic words that transform the discussion into a ask.)

There was hardly a moment's hesitation, "I think I can do that."

I don't have to read a book on fundraising to know I asked for too little! What to do? Stumbling right on top of his words, I said: "A million dollars a year, each year for the next three years."

"Well . . . I hadn't thought about doing anything like that, nothing that large."

I start probing with my four questions, the magic four questions. I am able to determine what the issue is. You would have come up with the same conclusion. He loves the college and the project. And actually, the amount I asked for isn't too much. I could have asked for more. It is the timing. That is it. He needs more time.

We finally settle on gift of $2.5 million spread over a five-year period. Dick would not have made that gift if I hadn't probed the question of timing.

A *yes* is a joy indeed, a flourish of trumpets. But be wary and concerned that you have not asked for enough. And the amount in Tommy's story is not what is significant in this example. That will seem to be a very major gift to some institutions. It was to this Methodist college. But we counsel our clients to use the same kind of probing and questions with their asks for $1,000 and $10,000. What happens if you ask for too much? You'll know when that happens—what I call the devastating crunch between your high expectations and the donor's resources and will.

Win Some, Lose Some

Let me tell you about another visit, one with a different ending.

I have called on Virginia several times in the past for other projects. We have developed a close relationship and exchange letters, phone calls, personal notes, and Christmas cards. In the past, she has been generous to each of my requests, a variety of worthy causes. This time I am talking with her about something I feel she would be particularly interested in.

I tell Virginia about the program and how much her gift will mean. I express the urgency and the need. I probe, I examine. Finally, I make the ask. (*"I would like you to consider . . ."*) And then, I pause. Remember, I admonish you to pause for as long as it takes.

But this time, the pause is intolerably long. Had I put Virginia to sleep? Had I stunned her into shock by the amount I asked? Is there cardiac arrest? I am about to reach for her wrist to see if there is still a pulse. Finally she says: "This is something I'll have to give some thought to. Why don't you leave the material and I'll give you a call."

Is this a *maybe* on its way to a *yes* or a *maybe* on its way to a *no*? Or perhaps a flat-out *no*?

Remember, you cannot leave the interview at this point without probing further. If you do, you'll understand nothing about the prospect's concerns, questions, and attitudes. And certainly, you don't want to leave the material and wait for a call.

What is Virginia really thinking? I begin the four questions. I discover the bad news when I probe the first question: Is it the institution? That was it. Precisely. Virginia had been giving small gifts to this organization on a regular basis, but she is a most generous person and gives to a number of institutions. I had it all wrong. I had given undue importance to these small gifts. It turns out she has no great passion for the organization.

Obviously, if I had left the material and waited for her to call me, as she requested, I would never have understood the situation. And worse, perhaps, I would never have heard from her.

It would have been possible to have spent a long time continuing to hold out hope for Virginia and plan for additional visits. I have known development directors who have called on prospects for years and have never gotten a gift. What Blake calls, "Faith over experience." Remember the old legal axiom? *To delay is to deny.* You somehow have to determine whether you are dealing with a viable prospect. If not, go on to the next one. There's a whole world waiting to give to you, simply waiting to be asked.

In the case of Virginia, she exercised the single most important reason why people do not make a major gift to a particular program: they simply do not believe in the mission of the institution. When you encounter that phenomenon, it is virtually impossible to turn the situation around. With great appreciation . . . take your leave . . . and go on to your next good prospect. In this case, Virginia and I remained good friends, and she has continued to give to a number of programs we discuss—but only those in which she is interested and has passion.

Some men and women find it extremely difficult to say *no*. Now mind you, they have no intention of making the gift—they simply have a difficult time saying so. And again, you need to probe to determine the kind of energy and time you will continue giving to this prospect. You listen carefully—not like the person I know who gives the impression: If I want your opinion, I'll give it to you!

Let me tell you the good news about all of this. But first, I'm reminded of that joke at the end of the movie *Annie Hall*. The guy goes to a doctor and says, "Doctor, I've got a terrible problem. My brother thinks he's a chicken." And the doctor says: "That's crazy. Just tell him he's not a chicken." And the guy says: "I can't. I need the eggs." Whenever I try to explain something that's entirely rational, I think of that.

Here's the good news. You're going to get the gift. You need not worry too much about technique or the "repeat after me-isms." You represent a great cause with inspiring solutions to human and social agendas. And you're calling on someone who is sensitive to the needs and your extraordinary service.

The important thing is that you ask.

And it's not enough to just begin. Persistence is what counts. Dogged perseverance. Your success depends on staying power. Robert Lowell called it: "Praying for the grace of persistence." The successful fundraiser, the one who gets the gift, is an apostle of faith and hope. (See, I told you this would be a sermon!) You condition the circumstances instead of being conditioned by them.

Ask!

Every study we have conducted, and every study I have seen, indicates that the reason people don't give is that they are not asked. But you already knew that.

Tear yourself away from the computer and your desk work. Make the contact. It's amazing what you don't get when you don't ask! I am profoundly convinced that it's not technique and slick salesmanship. Your job is truly simple: you create an understanding of the very special mission of your institution, and then secure the necessary funds to sustain that mission. That's what it's all about. Nothing more.

It has to do with human spirit and values, and dreams and high aspirations. Most of all, it means developing the trust and rapport with those you call on.

I've put on my hand to some uncontrolled doggerel that helps to better define the severity of the asking problem:

> A tired and haggard fundraiser
> Met the Devil at Hell's gate.
> What have you done, asked Satan,
> To earn this terrible fate?
>
> I don't know, the fundraiser said,
> I never shirked a task.
> I called on every prospect . . .
> I guess I failed to make the ask.
>
> The devil showed no mercy,
> With disgust he rang the bell.
> I condemn you to an eternity, he said,
> In the fires of deepest hell.

It takes the proper perspective. Getting the gift is not really a victory for the fundraiser, although there is high exultation. You want to sing the doxology. You hear the early chords of Beethoven's *Fifth*. But it's truly a victory for the donor and the institution. Everyone wins. And all it takes is the right person calling on the right prospect, for the right amount in the right way.

We have done some research on why people say *no* to a gift. This will be helpful to you. I won't bother with the details, but I'll give you just enough information to be a guide.

The most basic reason, and the one that is the most difficult to turn around, is that there is a mismatch of interest. Not even the high gods can make things be as if they have never been. The prospect simply lacks the passion and fervor for the institution.

Of great importance in not getting the gift is that there is a failure to convey a sense of urgency. The presentation may have been dramatic and appealing, near dazzling! But none of that was quite as important as providing a feeling that time will not wait, the gift must be made now in order to provide the solution to this exigent problem. If the issue isn't pressing, why should they give to you? There are so many other institutions, with hungry arms extended, demonstrating worthy, acute, and demanding opportunities for service.

I'll go on with my list.

Failure to ask for a specific amount is mentioned next in importance. Asking for a gift in a range (let's say, of $10,000 to $25,000), sends a signal to the prospect that you don't have a specific need. It says you haven't done your homework well enough to know precisely what amount you should ask for. And remember, when asking in a range, the floor inevitably becomes the ceiling.

Coupled or lined with the issue regarding "amounts" is that the prospect was asked for too much. This is not uncommon. Or, and this will surprise you, you asked for too little. In the latter, our study shows that people who are asked for less than they feel they can give believe that the project is not very important—because you did not press for an adequate amount.

In this business, we have an old, hoary, verity that claims that you can't ask a person for too much. We've been told for years that prospects will be complimented by an excessive ask. At least that's the dictum. Wrong! Just like most of those perfect fundraising guides, this one is plausible, hopeful, believable—and very wrong. You will find that in many cases when you ask for too much, you will not get a gift. Nothing! It will be easier for the prospect not to make a gift rather than donate a smaller amount that is felt to be disappointing to the institution or ego-minimizing to the person.

I'll tell you my worst experience in this regard. Don't let it happen to you. On a first visit with a gentleman in a small Western Pennsylvania community, I talked with him about a gift to the YMCA. He is zealous about the Y. There is no need for selling and certainly no need to press. There is a near-spiritual quality when he speaks about what the organization meant to him in his youth. We speak about a gift of ten thousand dollars, which for him is a stretch. But I ask him to consider taking extra time, perhaps five years, to extend the gift to $25,000.

We set a date for our next meeting. Before that visit, a board member convinces me that we should be asking for $100,000. He says I aimed too low. I didn't follow my instincts. I've been wrong before(!), but I should have known better.

On the second visit, I speak as ardently as possible about a gift of one hundred thousand dollars. He breaks down, in front of the board member and me. He loves the YMCA so much—and because he can't give the $100,000 we asked for, he feels he is letting the organization down. We had a very difficult time talking him back into giving the $25,000 I should have settled for on the first visit. He felt that the amount was a great disappointment to us. I won't let anyone talk me into doing that sort of thing again.

Another reason people don't give is that there is a mismatch of the solicitor. That may be you! You need to be certain that you are precisely the right one to make the call. If not, choose someone else. The chemistry needs to be right, and there has to be a sense of trust and rapport.

In all of my time, I have only known two exceptions to this next reason—a failure to include the spouse. Husbands and wives do discuss their philanthropy. Count on it. If you are seeking a major gift, you had better include the spouse. If you don't, there's a problem. The gift is going to be discussed by the husband and wife—and you won't be around to make your presentation.

And, finally, although our study universe didn't put it quite this way, they told us the request was fundraising-driven. By that, they meant that the person who made the presentation had spent all of their time talking about the goal, the giving boxes and ranges, how much they had yet to raise, and things of that sort. Nothing was said about what the gift would mean to the donor and how it would impact the lives of those touched and served by the organization.

The important lesson is that all of the reasons can be overcome, except the first (and perhaps even that), if sufficient cultivation is done through effective nurturing.

That's why the prospect and donor management system I described is so important. Adequate cultivation is essential. As they say, the more times you run over a cat, the flatter it gets.

I read a book the other day on salesmanship. There was a great deal that was relevant to our field. The author pointed out that 27% of the salesmen give up after the first objection by a prospect. An additional 11% give up after the second objection. But they discovered that 73% of the prospects voice two objections before buying the product. We know in our business that three *no's*, and you're half way to a *yes*. It's easy to give up, what Sir Thomas More refers to as "the loss of the soul." You must dare to stretch a tip-toe grasp for the golden ring and take the soaring ride of success.

I want to make a confession. I understand it's good for the spirit and cleanses the soul. When I first started in development (It was so long ago, we didn't call it development. It was just plain fundraising.), I was terrified to make the contact, the confrontation, and the ask. When I was twenty-three, in Lima, Ohio, and asked Paul Fisher for one hundred dollars, I was trembling. Well . . . the truth is, I nearly wet my pants. I finally blurted out the amount. He said: "Oh, I'll do better than that, Jerry, I'll give you a thousand dollars. Then he took out his billfold and started counting out twenty dollar bills. And I . . . I kept saying: "Oh, Paul, you don't really have to give that much, not really." I haven't made that particular mistake again!

For those few of you who are as fearful as I was—take heart. You really will get the gift you ask. Place your faith and courage in ideas, ideals, values, people, and the nobility of your great cause. I want you to exercise an un-clenching determination and irresponsible optimism. Give high definition to what is essential and relevant—make the ask and probe my four questions.

Be of high hope and faith unquenchable. Take the initiative, accept the challenge, lust for the adventure. Be willing to attack the bold and rewarding undertaking. This is what marks the truly successful. And to all the necessary qualifications, add only determination and plod. You'll get the gift.

FasTrack Tenets

Remember the **Four Magic Questions**. They're worth reviewing. In your sessions with a prospect, you must determine their level of interest in the institution and the project. And you have to find out whether the gift you ask for is at the right level and whether you have suggested the right timing.

1   If there is any lack of enthusiasm or affirmation, you need to find out if it is because of:

  The Institution

  The Project

  The Amount You Ask For

  The Timing

2   You should probe to determine if the amount you ask for is what the prospect had hoped or wanted to give. If it is, you may have to extend the amount of time that is required to make payments.

3   You cannot leave an interview without probing to determine the prospect's concerns, questions, and attitudes.

4   As I've noted, some people find it exceedingly difficult, and for some impossible, to say *no*. They will let you leave the interview thinking that they are interested and will make a gift. The next day you will receive a note with a small check or no check.

These people are the *smilers and nodders*. You cannot leave without finding out how they really feel.

5   Most important of all is that you ask for the gift. You ask!

6   Most people object before making their gift. Don't let the objections throw you. Use them to your advantage.

7
Listen The Gift

I felt miserable.

Jim Bowers and I were leaving Marianne's home. Leaving without the gift. Leaving without even a hope of getting it.

I can't remember when I have felt worse. It wasn't that we didn't get the gift—I've been on many calls where I've been disappointed. It was just that I felt so certain this time. We started the morning with such high hopes and expectations, Jim and I. We knew Marianne would make a large gift. We were certain.

We had an architect build a model. It was gorgeous. Everything was to scale. There was landscaping and the trees. There was even a reflecting pool. The model was huge, and with its glass top plenty heavy. It took both Jim and me to carry it into Marianne's living room. We placed it on her coffee table.

We had rehearsed this part pretty well. At just the right moment, we would pull the cover back—with a flourish, I might add. I had practiced that part myself.

I'll tell you the truth of it: I was so certain of the gift, I would've banked it.

What went wrong?

I'll get back to Marianne's story in just a bit. So that you don't feel unhappy through the rest of this chapter, I can tell you now that there's actually a happy ending.

Let me tell you first about a study I conducted for one of my books*. I interviewed forty men and women who I consider to be the greatest fundraisers in the country. It's possible that not all of them would be on your list of the greatest—but I can promise you that my group will be as good as any roster you come up with, and perhaps better.

I had in–depth interviews with each, usually lasting the whole day. And with a number, for more than a day.

I wanted to isolate the factors, attributes, and characteristics that go into making a really great fundraiser. I thought that if anyone could help me identify these skills and talents, my group could.

It was a fascinating journey. What made it all the more significant was the unanimity among my forty great fundraisers.

I must tell you that many of the talents that were identified as being of the most significant are innate. That's the unfortunate truth of it: You're born with most

*Born to Raise, Precept Press, 1991

of the important attributes. You either have them or you don't. You can't go to a seminar or read a book that will help you. Not even this book!

But the factor that was chosen as the second most important is one that can be learned. It was: *Listening*. My group was virtually unanimous on this characteristic. They rated it higher than persistence, appearance, persuasiveness, presence, speaking ability, salesmanship, and a host of other items.

I won't tell you now what is considered the most essential attribute. I'm sorry about that. You'll have to read *Born to Raise* to find that out!

Here's the important lesson. Assertive, creative, effective listening is a skill that can be learned. And it is the key to getting the gift.

Proper listening ensures you of getting as close to a successful ask as you possibly can. You can count on it.

Then why aren't there more seminars on listening, more books written on the subject? It can, after all, be learned.

Why isn't there more emphasis on listening? You've heard about fundraisers who talk too much. You've never heard of one who listens too much.

The most extraordinary lesson in fundraising took place over a hundred years ago at the old Blackstone Hotel in Chicago. It was 1889. Now mind you, that's over 110 years ago.

Frederick Taylor Gates, an ordained Baptist minister, led a successful effort to raise $400,000 to match a $600,000 grant from John D. Rockefeller. Gates' success in meeting the challenge made possible the creation of the University of Chicago.

Gates was meeting with a group of community leaders at the Blackstone. They asked how he managed to accomplish this unthinkable feat—raising $400,000. He gave them eighteen rules. Each is an absolute gem.

Listen to the wisdom. Keep in mind this is over one hundred years ago. And oh, one thing more: Gates refers to prospects as *victims*. I'm not so sure this is any worse than the depersonalized term we use all of the time: *Prospects*.

In any case, it's *victims*!

Here's what Gates told the group about getting the gift: "Let the victim talk freely, especially in the earlier part of the interview. While he is thus revealing himself, he is giving you the opportunity to study him and all his peculiarities. By the time he is through, you will be prepared, if you are alert, with your plan of successful attack.

"Never argue with a man, never contradict him. Never oppose anything he says that you are not absolutely bound to oppose by the very essential nature of your mission. In all else, yield. If your man is talkative, let him talk, talk, talk. Give your fish line and listen with the deepest of interest to every syllable.

What a remarkable explanation of *Listening the Gift*.

Of all of the communication functions, adults spend most of the time in listening activities. It is the least understood and the most undervalued function—but the most important. And it is the most easily learned and the simplest to hone to perfection.

In every day life, we spend over sixty-five percent of our waking hours in verbal communications—listening and talking. Those who study human behavior tell us that this is how time is allocated for all types of communications:

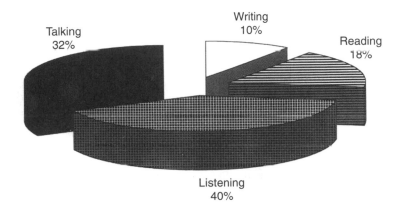

In asking for a major gift and in integrity fundraising, here's how the fundraiser should allocate the time:

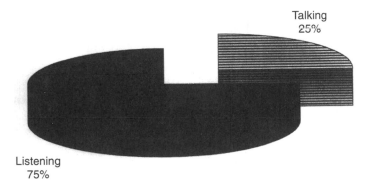

If you are spending more than twenty-five percent of your time talking during a visit, you're not *listening the gift*. You will never know what the prospect wants to tell you.

Have you ever been engaged in a conversation with someone when you were determined that you would spend all of your time listening, and not talking? Try it. Be absolutely intent that the person will talk and talk and talk. Rivet your attention.

I was in a session such as that recently. I went into the meeting determined I would do nothing but ask questions. We had over an hour of conversation. When it was finished, Betty Noyes said: *I can't remember when I have had such an enjoyable a time. This was great fun. Do come again.* Out of the hour, I doubt that I spoke more than five minutes, ten at the most.

When many fundraisers think of communications, the first thought is *sending*—talking one-on-one to donors, conversing in small groups, or speaking in front of an audience. But by far, the greatest percentage of our time, and the most important, should be in *receiving*—listening.

It may seem like a paradox but—the greater your ability to listen, the more likely the other person will listen to you.

Your prospect is much like you. They have as much interest, or as little, in your particular story as you have in theirs. But it's not your prospect's job to get information from you and to listen to you. It's the other way around. You *listen the gift.*

When you feel the urge to regale the prospect with your own wonderful story, or perhaps an improved version of what the prospect is telling—stop. **Stop!** Just think of why you're together.

What To Do When In Doubt

It often shows your effective command of the language—to say nothing. Keep in mind my colleague-consultant Karen Hamilton's admonition: "Snap your fingers to the beat of some rap music and repeat—'When in doubt, shut your mouth, when in doubt . . .'"

Here are some general guidelines that will help hone your listening skills. They will help ensure your success in getting the gift—at the right time and at the right level.

1   If you find yourself talking more than 20 to 25 percent of the time, there's a good chance you will never hear the prospect telling you how he or she feels about the institution and what he or she wants to give to it. Or what objections there may be. You will never know what their greatest needs and desires are. Stop talking and *listen the gift.*

2   What you don't know about your prospect, and his or her interests and passions, will hurt you in getting the gift. What you do know will only help you.

Keep in mind that everything is important in the business of listening. What you hear is not always what is being communicated. You have to take into consideration the tone, the emphasis, the gestures, and the body language.

The prospect's facial expressions, the gestures, the eye contact—will help you *listen* to some things that aren't said!

3   Listen with intensity. Listen with your eyes as well as your ears. You must be acutely attuned to the

prospect's tone, the emotional tenor, and the context of the situation. These all merge to provide a direction.

The uninitiated fundraiser rushes in and doesn't wait long enough to absorb and assimilate the entire communication. Instead, there is a big swallow at the first piece of conversational bait. What is finally caught are bits and pieces, not really worthwhile, so insignificant that they get thrown back—often at a confused prospect.

4 Learn how to ask effective questions. Practice. This is no time for impromptu training. Asking unerring questions is a delicate balance between getting the gift and simply having a good time. Probing and asking the right questions in precisely the right way is the difference between flying or just flapping your wings.

There are some techniques and gestures you can practice and learn. But in the end, good listening depends on asking the right question. And there's nothing more effective than asking . . . *What do you think about that?*

5 You get the lines of making a successful ask hopelessly tangled if you have the need to talk too much, too often. Remember: You need to *Listen the Gift.*

When you spend most of the time in the discussion talking, it's very difficult to remember everything that you said. And the prospect won't remember. Worse, the purpose of the meeting is to find out what the prospect's needs and interests are.

6   After each meeting with a prospect, attach a sheet to your *Call Report*. (Shame! Haven't you been doing *Call Reports*? Start now.) Respond to the following questions: Were my comments relevant and persuasive? Am I taking the prospect one step closer to a an investment? Is my objective totally in place? Was I clear about what I wanted to achieve in the discussion? Did I gain additional information about the prospect? If the answer is no to any of these questions, you weren't listening effectively.

7   Interrupting or finishing a statement for someone is comparable to stomping on their toes. It may make you feel better, but you will learn nothing. And it hurts the other person terribly.

8   You listen for the little things. You listen for everything. All bits and pieces add to your reservoir of information. Every scrap becomes important.

Listening to your prospect can provide valuable insight into his or her character, interests, and needs. Listen assertively and you will be a step closer to your successful ask.

You never know when there exists that precise and precious moment when there can be a turning in the intent and interest. If your mind wanders away from the objective at hand, if you relax for even an instant your intense concentration—your fundraising mission is bound to falter. You lose!

9   Relax. Be patient.

Let your prospects finish before you respond. Keep in mind that they may have dealt some of their top cards. But they may be ready in just a moment to play their trump. Give them time to show their total hand, or you won't be playing with a full deck.

Even your mother taught you that you are blessed with two ears and one mouth—a constant reminder that you should listen twice as much as you talk.

10   For the level of intense, assertive listening I'm recommending, make your presentation in a place where physical and mental distractions are minimal. You want to be certain you can be heard and understood, just as you want to be sure you can hear everything.

Let me create a scene for you. You'll understand what I mean. You and the prospect are in a busy, noisy, trendy, chi-chi restaurant.

You: *And so I thought you would be interested in this special project. We are going to bring together all of our equipment and facilities and pool all of our people.*

Prospect: {leaning forward} *Fool our people? For what?*

You: *No—pool them. What we want to do is a better job. Cooperation.*

Prospect: {cupping one hand to the ear} *Corroboration? Are you calling me a liar?*

You: *Good grief! Did you say the place is on fire?*

Prospect: *You're right, I am tired. Why don't we get together at another time?*

11   It is important that you ask open-ended questions. Regularly along the way, you need to test whether the person is listening and absorbing. You need to probe the level of their interest.

One way of finding this out (the wrong way!) is to ask a direct question such as: "Do you find the kind of program I've just described interesting?" That may end up getting you just a *yes* or *no*. If it's a firm *no*, you may not have to go any further! But if the response is *yes*, followed by a long silence—where do you go from there?

A better question than, "Do you find this interesting?" is: "Tell me how you feel about the program I've just described." That kind of a question is going to require more than a simple *yes* or *no*.

I find it extremely helpful to indicate that we don't have all of the answers and that we seek the prospect's counsel. Try something such as this: "We're not entirely certain as to what our most effective direction ought to be. What do you think we should do?" I remind you that this is an open-ended question that can't be answered by *yes* or *no*. Here's another probe that is certain to get a response. "What do you suggest we do now, how do we proceed with this idea?"

Some other good opportunity openers you may wish to use are comments such as:

Please tell me more about that

I'd like to hear what you're thinking

It sounds like you have some real feeling about that

I'd really be interested in hearing what you have to say about that

12   It may seem trite, you've heard it so often—but criticism and objections are truly your best friends.

I have been through a number of sessions where the person I'm calling on is smiling and nodding his or her head in perfect harmony with the wondrous words I am using to describe the project. I never stopped to ask the right questions. I was too madly in love with my own golden words. The person was nodding and smiling. But internally, they were saying—*no*.

These are the worst kinds of sessions because when the session is closing and the prospect tells you, *I just want a little more time to think it over*—you may feel you've made the sale. All of that smiling and nodding!

Wrong!

Probe for any possible concerns, questions, or criticisms. "Do you feel as good about this program as I believe you do?" or, "This is important, isn't it?" If there are concerns, respond by asking the right questions . . . and then listening.

Am I correct that this is the problem as you see it?

What I understand you to say is . . .

As I understand it from what you say, you feel the problem is . . . (restatement of problem)

Am I hearing you correctly? This is how you feel . . .

Here are the key issues you mentioned as I understand them.

Please tell me about it.

13   Should you record when you are talking with the prospect? Of course not. That would be unthinkable.

Should you take notes? Only if you need to record detailed information, specific items or answers for your next meeting. Or perhaps when designing a Planned Gift. Otherwise, I suggest no written notes at the session. Remember, you are engaging someone in a joyous conversation.

What you will find, and this is fascinating, is that the better listener you become, the better your memory. Somehow as you concentrate on your listening, your memory kicks into high gear. You remember everything. It is as if there is total recall. You are a sponge.

14   When you are with your potential donor, keep in mind what he or she is saying to you. They're not, of course, saying it out loud—but I promise you, this is what they're thinking. I'd like you to review this before your call. Consider it. Think about it. Here's what your prospect is saying:

I'm asking you to listen to me and I have the feeling you are trying to convince me of something. But you keep stomping on my thoughts and sensitivities. You're not solving my problem if you're talking—because you won't know what my problem is. Please listen to me, that's all I ask. If you make it seem like it's my idea, I am more likely to agree. If you make me feel it is my dream, I'm more willing to become a partner with you. If you don't ask, you won't know how I feel. If you don't probe, you won't understand my strong feelings. Listen to me: I want to save the world. But you'll never know that if you keep talking.

It has changed. The effective fundraiser of the past was a person who knew how to sell and tell. (Some would say *slick*. That would probably be the worst possible description you would want to hear.) These were the fundraisers of the past, like the pizza man: make it, bake it, take it. Boom!

The effective fundraiser of the future will be the person who knows how to listen, and therefore motivate. The successful fundraiser of the future will *listen the gift*.

This will demand an excellence and a quality not often practiced in the past. It will require you to surpass the peak of your powers. The new age will not accept second best. Listening is the insertion of a creative and inspiring interaction between a brief presentation and encouraging the prospect to talk.

Oh, yes. I want to finish the story about Marianne, the story with the horrible beginning and the happy ending.

You may remember that I made the call with James Bowers. Jim is one of the most effective fundraisers I have ever worked with. In our thinking and planning, we were convinced that Marianne would be interested in the Women's Pavilion of a major medical center. All of our presentation and the architect's model was geared to that. We were certain she would find it exciting.

She didn't.

During our presentation, Marianne was *out to lunch.* Her eyes were glazed.

Jim was smart enough not to ask for the gift. We gathered up all of our material and carried the architect's model back to Jim's office. It was a lot heavier going back than it was going in! We felt sunk.

Jim said: "Let's make a list of everything we heard. Marianne did a great deal of talking and we were good about our listening." We heard plenty.

Marianne told us about her father who founded one of the major corporations in the country. She talked about how her father had raised her and how devoted she was to her dad, head-over-heels in love with him.

And then we talked about something that Jim and I had not really known. Her father was an alcoholic. There were many evenings when Marianne had to help him to bed and tuck him in.

We were told that her father had left a large estate. We knew that—to the dollar! But of particular interest, Marianne told us that her father had been very generous during his lifetime, but nothing had ever been named for him.

Now that would tend to get the attention of a fundraiser!

Find The Right Button

When Jim and I had completed our list of what we had heard, it became very obvious to us. You would have come to precisely the same conclusion. The Women's

Pavilion was not the right button. What Marianne would be interested in would be an alcohol treatment center, which was also part of the overall plan for the medical center—a facility to be named for her family.

There's much more to the story and how we put the pieces together. We called on Marianne again and asked for her support to build the new alcohol treatment center. Her gift was $3 million.

I'd like to take some credit for the gift. But neither Jim nor I really deserve it. We were not persuasive at all. We simply *listened the gift*. Any one of you would have heard and done the same.

Arthur Rubinstein was once asked by an ardent admirer: "How do you handle the notes as well as you do?" The pianist answered: "I handle the notes no better than many others, but the pauses—ahh! That is where the art resides." In getting the gift the art is in the listening.

One more word about that wonderful woman. Marianne and I have become dear friends. She reminds me of what Marilou Awiabeta wrote in *Abiding Appalachia*: "Creation often needs two hearts—one to root and one to flower." That's Marianne—both hearts dwell in one lovely person.

Whenever, I see Marianne, she never fails to thank me for making the gift possible. Thank me! That's something else I have discovered in all of the research I have done: The great joy people feel in making their gifts. And Marianne, all that extraordinary woman wants is to save the world. And she is having a wonderful, joyous time doing it.

And that's the reward and fulfillment for us, also—we fundraisers. We enable and empower all of this to happen. We do it for our great causes and missions—by *listening the gift.*

Just remember what your mother taught you: Be seen and not heard.

FASTRACK TENETS

1   If you find yourself talking more than twenty-five percent of the time, chances are you'll never hear what the prospect is trying to tell you. You won't know what he or she wants to give to or what objections there may be. Listen the gift.

2   What you don't know about the prospect will hurt you. What you do know will work to your great advantage.

3   Listen with intensity. Listen with your eyes as well as your ears.

4   Learn how to ask effective questions. Probe. Examine. Most of all, good listening depends on asking the right questions.

5   The prospect will not remember everything you said. In fact, they'll remember very little. They will remember what they said. Remember, the purpose of the meeting is to find out the prospect's needs and interests.

6   Determine after every visit whether you have helped the prospect come closer to making a gift. Put it in writing. Indicate whether you achieved your objectives for the meeting.

7   Listen for the little things. Everything counts. It provides the valuable insights to the prospect's character, interests, and needs.

8   Be patient. Relax. Let your prospect finish before you respond. Don't interrupt or finish their statements.

9 Make your presentation in a site where physical and mental distractions are minimal.

10 Ask open-ended questions. Be certain to test throughout the visit whether the person is truly listening and absorbing your comments. Keep probing for the level of their interest.

11 Be certain to probe for any concern or problems that might exist. If you don't examine, you'll never know how the prospect really feels.

12 It is best not to record or take notes during the visit.

13 You'll never know what the prospect really wants if you keep talking. If you make them feel it is their dream, they are more willing to become a partner with you.

8

The More You Talk,
The Less You Learn

Some things just seem to work like magic. That's the way it was when Bill Sturtevant and I founded the Institute for Charitable Giving. Today, it is regarded as one of the nation's most significant centers for training and coaching major gift and planned giving officers. We find, also, that volunteers seem to benefit every bit as much from the seminars.

Bill and I have both preached that *listening* is where securing the gift at the proper level actually begins. Because we felt so strongly on the matter, we devised a guide for listening, and then put it into the form of a self-evaluation.

You've never seen anything as comprehensive and penetrating. I know, because we searched and searched. That's why we finally developed our own. I'll cover some of the salient guidelines in a moment. I've also included a copy in the Appendix of this book.

But first let me tell you what happens at some of our seminars. We ask those in the group who feel they are *good listeners* to identify themselves. Usually, there are fewer than a handful out of a large group. Sometimes no one volunteers. Then we ask the few that do consider themselves good listeners to come up to the front of the room to join Bill and me.

We start asking questions. (That's what good listeners do!) We all agree that listening is not inherent. That's important for you to understand. No one says that they were born that way. They tell us they work at it. Listening is an attribute that you learn, practice, and work at. Everyone agrees that listening is one of the most important characteristics of the a successful fundraiser.

We ask the group if they feel they are effective listeners. Most say they are. Then we ask them to take the test. That's when there's a moment of truth—as Hemingway said: "When perception meets damnable reality." Try it. See for yourself. After you finish the chapter, turn to the Appendix and take the test. What we know is that if you're not listening, you're not learning.

David Ogilvy, the giant and singular doyen of the advertising world, is the master of motivating people. He says that one of the most crucial jobs for all of us is to be a good listener. "So much of the art of communications is the ability to listen. That has everything to do with motivating people."

I want to relate a fascinating story. It is one of the best examples of listening I have ever heard. It helps punch through the state of the art. Before the story, let me tell you a little bit about the science of hearing. Hearing, by the way, is not listening. Don't confuse the two.

Dr. Albert Mehrabian is a noted authority on listening. He says that people *hear* what you are saying through a combination of many factors. What comes next may surprise you (it did me). Dr. Mehrabian says that fifty-five percent of what is heard comes from facial expressions, posture, gestures, and eye contact. The tone of the voice conveys an additional thirty-eight percent of what people *hear*. And a lowly seven percent comes from the actual words.

That's the lesson. A prospect may tune you out, no matter how glorious your presentation—because of a certain look, a shift to a stern or closed posture, or some gesture that is off-putting.

At the same time, it's important that you watch carefully the facial expressions and the gestures of those you are calling on. Look for those tell-tale signs. There may be the special movements of the lips, the cheek muscles, and the eyebrows. Dr. Mehrabian says these reveal a great deal about what is going on inside the person. Be particularly aware of expressions that convey tension, doubt, and lack of attention.

And now my story. I am calling on Frank to discuss the program at Tower School in Marblehead, Massachusetts. Frank's son and a grandson have attended Tower, and he's a prospect for a gift. Tower is a very special independent grade school lead by Dr. James Bonney. Jim knows a thing or two about cultivation. When I first met Jim, he was greeting parents at their cars as they were dropping off their kids. That left an impression I'll never forget. Jim would open the door, greet the youngster and the parent. And always a special word, some encouragement, a question about the family. Every day. Rain or Snow.

Now back to Frank and my story. He says: "Let me tell you about someone who knows something about fundraising. I get a call the other day from Neil. (Dr. Neil L. Rudenstine is President of Harvard University.)

"He didn't have an assistant call or a secretary. He makes the call himself. 'Frank,' he says, 'I'm having lunch two weeks from Thursday in my office with a few friends, and I want you to join us. I think you will know most of them.'

"Now that really gets my attention. I get a call direct from the President of Harvard. That's a call you have to take. He says he wants me to join a few friends for lunch in his office. Not in some special dining room or at a club, but in his office. That's impressive. And only a few are coming. That makes me feel kind of special.

"Well, even though there's not much advance notice, I clear my schedule of another engagement. I drive to Cambridge, and find the President's office. I've been there before. It was just as he said, there were about a half a dozen men there, and I knew two or three of them.

"It was a wonderful lunch. Not very fancy, but very special. Do you know what I mean? A big round table with a checkered table cloth, kind of like a *French picnique*. Some French bread, cheese, wine, and a delightful entrée.

"We have about thirty minutes of lively conversation. Neil talks about what's happening at the University and his vision for the future. He's quite a guy. Then we were surprised by what came next.

"Neil says: 'I've brought you together today to ask your advice.' (Pretty darn good strategy, Frank says. That's a great way to get a person's attention.) I need your help. I have been charged to lead this great University, a true cathedral of academics and learning. I know you all love the University. You have shown it in so many ways in the past.

" 'But I have to ask this question. In the past few years, in the case of each of you, you have stopped giving to the University. We will always love you just as much, whether you give or not. But I have to ask you why, why did you stop giving?' "

Frank tells me that in his own case, he had been giving several hundred thousand dollars a year. He stopped giving because . . . well, because he felt that the University really didn't need the money as much as some of his other activities. Not that the University was less worthy, only that they didn't need it as much. He says that he mentioned it at the meeting during the group discussion.

Frank tells me that the entire discussion was joyful, light, and lively. These were all men who had given at least one hundred thousand dollars a year on a regular basis to the University, but for some reason had stopped giving in the past few years.

Frank goes on. "The President was magnificent. He has a very special way of riveting on the person who is talking. He kept taking notes. Lots of notes. I was impressed with that. No matter how inconsequential some of the comments were, the President took notes of it, and kept punctuating with his own comments such as: 'This is terribly important information for me,' or 'I'm so glad you told me that.' A couple of times he told us we should have called him direct when we had that kind of question.

"Me, I told the President I had stopped giving because I didn't think my gift, even several hundred thousand dollars a year, was important considering how much Harvard was raising each year. He jumped on that. He was quick to tell me how critically important it was, how every gift was significant to the University, how greatly they depended on philanthropy.

"Then another person tells about how his nephew was not admitted to the University. The President explains how it would have been impossible for him to interfere with the admission process, but that perhaps the nephew made a better choice. 'The truth is,' the President says, 'I couldn't get into Harvard myself today. It's really pretty difficult. He probably got into a school that was a better choice for him.'

"Another person talks about not getting the right football tickets. Here the President says that he really could have done something about that. 'Why didn't you tell me, why didn't you give me a call? Here, let me give you my private line.' We all make note of the President's private line.

"And on it goes. And on. By the end of the discussion, we had all become roaring converts and advocates, absolute zealots for the University.

"We're all queuing up to thank the President for the wonderful luncheon. I overhear the guy in front of me saying: 'And Neil, you can count on me again for my couple hundred thousand dollars this year.' And I'm saying the same thing to the President.

"I'll tell you what really got us all. It was the way the President listened and really seemed to want our advice. That's what did it. He really seemed interested and concerned. I think we are all back into making our gifts."

Some Lessons Here

Think of what the President did to make this session so monumentally effective. It began with the small group. He made them feel the selection was very exclusive. (He probably did a dozen small groups—but each was felt by the invitees to be special and exclusive.) My own experience in doing a number of similar sessions since hearing of this one at Harvard is that they work best of all when there are no more than nine present—almost always the chief executive officer, perhaps another staff person as a keen and quiet observer, a listener to take notes—and a maximum of seven prospects or donors. (As Aristotle said, "There is a divinity in odd numbers.")

Somehow, I find that it doesn't seem to work as well with a much smaller group. There isn't the synergy, the building of consensus, the discussion, the excitement, the ability of the chief executive officer to respond in such a way that there is the true sense of gathering information and receiving guidance.

Try it. It really works. I've done it so many times now that it has become part of an ongoing strategy in many of our programs. Soon after I had heard about the Harvard experience, we tried it at the Albert Einstein Medical Center—with the same exciting and productive results.

Raymond Alexander was the chief executive officer. He had an extraordinary way of probing, asking questions, showing great concern, and expressing deep appreciation for the input. Remember, this isn't show and tell for the staff. This is an honest attempt to listen.

Let me tell you about Ray at one of our early sessions. I still remember it clearly. There are four couples, Ray, and I. I am there to listen, observe, take notes, and determine the next appropriate steps.

Here's Ray: "I have asked you to come here this evening for dinner and a brief discussion . . . because I really need your help. (A great beginning. People love helping someone they highly regard, and they love giving their opinion and advice.)

"We have just completed a major campaign for Albert Einstein and the truth is . . . well, the truth is that you folks didn't give as much as we thought you would want to (note: He didn't say, *as much as you ought to give*), and some of you didn't even make a gift. We know you love the hospital. You have shown it in so many ways. And we know that you are grateful to Albert Einstein.

"You, Sarah and Ben, your four children were born here. And Samuel, you had your open heart surgery here. It's fair to say that your life was saved right here at Albert Einstein." And on it went until he had circled the group.

Then Ray says: "Now tell me, where did we go wrong? There must be some way that we have disappointed you. I need to know. We shall never love you less for what you have done or haven't done. But I am in charge of this hospital, and I need to know where I have let you down." (I like this approach. It's not that,

"You have let us down," but rather, "Where have I disappointed you?")

The responses were extraordinary. Virtually all were personal and quite picky. The billing was incorrect or hard to understand. The admitting took too long. They had misspelled Ben's name. And on it went.

Ray responded with deep concern and assured them that they should have called him direct. He gave them the number of his private line and made them promise that they would call the next time anything like this happened.

In the case of Albert Einstein, we conducted sessions just like this for a total of thirty-six couples. Out of that group, twenty-seven followed within a month with a gift, most of them of six-figures.

It will work for you. You suspend your own agenda and desire to talk. You listen, assertively and intently. I have used the same process in dozens of situations and it has never failed. It is what Aristotle must have meant when he spoke about the genius behind the initiation of a desired action.

What we emphasize with the chief executive officer we work with on these meetings is that we are not selling—we are gathering information and listening. Listening. Listening. In the end, the better you understand, the easier it will be to get the gift.

These meetings deserve an immediate follow-up letter from the chief officer, thanking the attendee for taking time for the visit. We find it a good technique, also, to do a summary of the discussion, which should be followed within a week.

Then most important, you call on the person or the couple for a follow-up visit. That's when the exploration for the gift begins. If there is no follow-up visit, you might as well have not planned the sessions in the first place. The follow-up visit is essential, like ketchup on a hamburger.

Just try to find a book on *listening*. There are plenty on *hearing*—but that is an entirely different phenomenon. If hearing is the science, the vibrations, the channels, the sound waves—*listening* is truly the art. That's where the meaning is.

I discovered through my research that listening is the second most important attribute in the fundraiser's bag of tools. Most important for us in the field, it's one that can be learned. I began searching for a book on the subject. I could find nothing. Nothing. If it is so important, why hasn't more been written about it? Why is it impossible to find good documentation?

I decided to search for, explore, and pursue—in any way possible—more information on listening. I wanted to prepare a compendium on this topic that is so vitally important to us in the field. I was obsessed! If this is so important, I would at least make a start. I do not get ideas—ideas get me. The more I thought about the compendium on listening, the more I was seized with the need.

A Certain Kind Of Listening

I couple the word *assertive* with *listening*. That says it all: *assertive listening*. I feel it best exemplifies the level of aggressive, positive, proactive, and compulsive listening that I have in mind. I want you to become a pushy listener!

Let's get *hearing* out of the way. We won't have to return to the subject. *Hearing* is an immensely complex and sophisticated phenomenon. It's the physical condition that permits sound to be received by the ear.

The ear is an elaborate labyrinth composed of vibrating fine bones and fluids. It accepts sound waves from the outer ear and sends them through a middle ear, and into the inner ear. There are sensitive nerves that transmit the message to the brain. All of this is a passive, and unconscious, act that takes place. I didn't really know any of that. I looked it up in my old college anatomy text which I dug out of a box in the basement.

But *listening*, is entirely different. Listening gives the *hearing* its meaning. It is a marvel. In the listening process, all of the thinking, assessing, reasoning, and responding takes place. Think of how vital that is to you, the fundraiser. Listening involves a mental and emotional activity of the highest order.

Here's the sad news. A recent exhaustive study confirmed that the average person listens with only twenty-five percent efficiency. That means that everything else that is spoken is typically heard and not absorbed. It gets worse. The twenty-five percent may not even fully register in the consciousness.

Think of your dazzling presentation, the one you prepared and practiced to perfection. The average person can recall only fifty percent of what he or she immediately hears. The study was conducted only minutes after they had heard it. And only eight hours later, one-half to one-third of the remainder is forgotten.

It's fascinating stuff, this business of listening. The average person talks at a maximum of two hundred words a minute. But people think at a rate of four hundred to five hundred words a minute. It's a problem because it leaves a tremendous amount of time for *daydreaming*. If a prospect isn't fully concentrating, you're in trouble.

Here is my *Compendium on Assertive Listening*. In all of the research I have done, I haven't found anything as extensive or complete. It certainly doesn't exhaust the topic, but it is a good beginning. I told my publisher that I would like to do another book, a book on *Assertive Listening*. He said it wouldn't sell. He said it doesn't sound very exciting. But what does he know about fundraising!

Compendium On Assertive Listening

1   We have two ears and one mouth. That probably means that God wanted us to listen twice as much as we speak. When you talk instead of listen:

- You are not learning anything about the prospect, his or her needs and desires.

- You will not hear any concerns because you are not probing.

- You will not uncover any giving-clues.

- You will not understand what he or she is willing to invest in.

- You may raise negative issues that the prospect had not thought of.

- You do not allow the prospect to gain ownership. There is no process for empowerment.

- You provide more opportunity for your prospect to disagree with you on some of your statements.

- You dominate the conversation instead of guiding it.

- You do not put a spotlight on the prospect and give him or her center stage.

- You do not give yourself breathing time to think ahead.

The more you talk, the less you learn. Listening is important because it is everything in gaining the gift.

2   Prospects are much more apt to respond to the questions that you pose than to the information you give them. This is true no matter how eloquent the presentation. By questioning, you understand how your prospect thinks and feels. It helps you get inside them. To do that effectively, you must use you ears, eyes, and sometimes your touch. Eye contact is very important and body language is, also. Research shows that all of this is as important as the words you use.

3   The more you talk the less you listen. And the more you talk, the less others listen.

There are some in the field who simply can't stop talking. They chatter away. It can be traced to nervousness, insecurity, and high apprehension. This style of fundraising communication, monopolizing the discussion, becomes more and more one-sided until in effect the fundraiser is talking to him- or herself. It is one of the great truths in our business that you show the most effective command of the language by saying nothing.

Let me tell you about my first session with Malin Burnham. Malin has since become a close and dear friend, but that first visit did not augur well a future relationship.

Malin is considered one of San Diego's most prominent leaders, a volunteer and a philanthropist of major note. He is also one of those people God touched in a special way. He is handsome, energetic, and a superb athlete in every sport he attempts. He's one of those people whose socks would never dare fall down, not on Malin Burnham!

I make my first visit with a volunteer who knows Malin well. Before we sit down, I notice some photographs on the wall. Malin had been on the crew that headed one of the successful America's Cup entries. The photos on the wall give testimony to his pride in being involved. He later went on to chair and sponsor several other winning Cup entries.

Before I can ask Malin any questions about his passion for sailing, the volunteer starts: "I love sailing. I go out every weekend and every time possible when I can." There followed twenty minutes of unstoppable and detailed exposition of how much the volunteer enjoyed sailing. As much as I tried to politely interrupt, there wasn't an opportunity to ask Malin about his great successes and victories.

What a horrible lost opportunity. We left the meeting gaining no information at all about how Malin felt about the project and whether this would be an area in which he would want to make an investment of his talents and treasure. I called on him later by myself. This time, Malin did all of the talking. We have remained close friends and keep in regular touch. He did, by the way, make a major gift to the project and accepted the chairmanship of the program.

4   The more attentive you are in listening to others, the more likely they will listen to you. Give your undivided attention to the person. Undivided! This sends a message that he or she is special, respected, and valued. When you demonstrate that you hold your prospect in high regard, you will get the very best out of them.

5   Listening is the most grievously overlooked and minimized characteristics in our skill chest—our repertoire of attributes. And of all the skills and talents, it is the one that can be most easily learned.

6   The person asking the questions is in control of the conversation. Think about that: It is not the person talking, but rather the person listening who is in charge. An attorney, for instance, examining and probing a witness is a prime example of what I'm talking about. They question, they probe, they examine, they direct the interrogation, the content of what the judge and jury hears, and they understand that the only dumb question is the one you don't ask. The person who listens influences the outcome, not the talker.

A wise old owl sat on an oak,
The more he saw, the less he spoke,
The less he spoke, the more he heard.

Why aren't we fundraisers like that
  wise old bird?

7   If you are in fundraising, you are in the listening
    business. It's what you do for a living—you are a lis-
    tener.

    This is a very small matter but it helps prove the
    point. I was with Irene Bailey this summer. She is
    the wife of John S. Bailey, President of the American
    College of Greece. I haven't see Irene for several
    years, but I noticed that she had a new ring that I
    hadn't seen before. I commented on it. "How in the
    world would you notice such a small thing? It's been
    two years since I saw you last." I told her that I no-
    ticed because I am in the business of listening and
    observing.

    For me, everything registers. There isn't a detail I
    miss. My wife might tell you otherwise but that's
    around the house. "You never noticed the new chair
    in the living room. You have been walking around it
    for two months."

8   Nonverbal signals are being sent when you talk to a
    prospect. You need to be aware of them. They tell
    you a great deal more about your prospect's true
    feelings and intentions than the words that he or she
    speaks.

    Words can lie, although this isn't usually the case in
    talking with a prospect. But they can unintentionally
    misguide. Those in the field say that only a third of
    the meaning is actually expressed through words.
    The remainder is provided through nonverbal com-
    munication. Experts say that the nonverbal is one

that is the most reliable. This means that you listen with your eyes.

9   This may sound strange, but *assertive listening* is getting the other person to agree with you. You win them to your side by listening. It is not your eloquence or your charmed words. It is listening that does the trick. Assertive listening. It is an art. And you are the artist. You become the assertive listener.

10   I call listening the hidden side of communications. That's because it seems that everybody wants to talk, but few want to listen. History records that our strongest leaders were great listeners. It is one of the keys to being a powerful leader.

11   Be certain the prospect is seated. That's usually not very difficult in the kind of situation fundraisers normally face. We are seated, relaxed, and carrying on a conversation. That would be a typical scenario.

Be on the alert. It isn't always the case but if a person moves about a great deal in the chair or begins standing, it usually means that they are rushed or impatient. It's a clue that you ought to gather all of your material and arrange for another visit at a better time. Sitting down puts both you and your listener at the same eye level, which makes it easier to maintain good eye contact.

12   We were shopping the other day for a new automobile. We walked into the show room and a perfectly nice sales person began singing the virtues of one of his cars. We had a twenty minute discourse on gas consumption, displacement, gear ratios, safety features, comprehension, and motor efficiency. Not

once did he stop to ask us any questions. He had absolutely no idea of what we might be interested in.

We drove thirty miles to another showroom of the same make automobile. There we had a sales person who spent fifteen or twenty minutes peppering us with questions. She wanted to know about our needs, the size of the family, what we had in mind, the amount and type of traveling we did, and so forth. By the time she finished, she seemed to know precisely the car we wanted. Surprise! And we bought the car.

Most prospects won't really listen or pay attention to what you are trying to sell until they are absolutely convinced that you have heard and appreciated their point of view. They want to be heard.

Your objective is, of course, to win the gift. The most effective way to make an impact is to have the prospect interpret his or her point of view before you present yours.

Simply stop. Suspend your agenda. Listen to all the prospect has to say and understand how he or she thinks and feels.

Make certain the prospect feels understood and appreciated. Montaigne said that what a person wants most in life is to be appreciated.

Make it a give-and-take process. But as far as you're concerned, it's mostly take. The most effective way to *feel* the gift is to make the other person feel listened to.

13   It's worth repeating: hearing is not listening. It is easy for the prospect to hear what you are saying. But that doesn't mean that he or she is really listening.

I'll tell you about Ken. It's a good example of what I have in mind. He was hearing, but not listening. Here's the story.

Ken and I had a great relationship. The chemistry was special. Not close friends, but the kind of association that was easy and comfortable.

I could call most any time for a visit or lunch. He would accept on the spot. I had been talking with him about a major gift to his alma mater. He could do it. His net worth was high, probably one of the most significant of any of the alumni. His annual income, in the last report I saw, was $3 million plus mighty handsome bonus arrangements.

His interest in the university coupled with his financial resources was . . . well, it was all enough to cause palpitations in the heart of a fundraiser. But more than that, Ken had spirit and soul as large as his bank account.

I called on him regularly to talk about the university. You're not supposed to have a visit unless there's a clear purpose and objective. I know that. I always know exactly where I am going with my discussions and my probing.

Each visit was built on to the next that followed. But nothing was happening. I was making no progress fast.

Somewhere along the line it occurred to me. Ken either has a very poor memory or he hasn't been listening to my eloquent words. If something like this has ever happened to you, try something that I used with Ken. It may help.

"Ken, you have been wonderful to meet with. These visits have been very meaningful for me. It occurs to me, however, that you haven't remembered some of the items we have talked about. I worry that I may have failed you. I certainly don't expect you to agree on every point, but your evaluation is so important to me that I would like some feedback. Here are some of the things we've discussed . . ."

It worked. And it was just as I guessed. He really hadn't been listening. Worse still, when he did listen at this session, he really wasn't excited about the project. But at least I learned without going through a number of additional visits.

I still care greatly for Ken. I don't judge people on the basis of what they give. He'll always be a friend. But I'm not certain he'll be the major donor I had hoped for. I'll spend my time for fundraising with other prospects, and my personal time with Ken. Some day, he may come around. But I don't fool myself—that won't be the rationale for my visits.

If you feel that your prospect is not listening carefully, or is listening selectively, you can direct the conversation to what you want to talk about by using one of these two strategies:

Ask an indirect question that requires a response: "What do you think about the hospital's idea of building a new cancer center?"

Or summarize what you've said, emphasizing what you think might have been ignored: "We've talked about the university's plans for the new learning center, and I felt that you sense that this was something that was quite important for our future growth. I would like to hear how you feel about the program."

14   Work on your voice, really work on it. It's hard to listen at length to someone whose voice is lacking in enthusiasm and energy. Equally annoying is having to strain to hear a soft voice or having to ask someone to repeat what has been said because of poor enunciation. A prospect may see your mouth moving, but doesn't absorb a word you are saying. Inflect your voice, vary the volume, the rate of speed, and put some real zest in what you say.

15   You are going to have times that your prospect is unhappy about one thing or another with the organization. It can be tough. I've had some, as they say, who are experts on everything, and generally wrong on almost everything.

Acknowledging the concern is not necessarily agreeing to its worthiness. You may use acknowledgment phrases to recognize the position and the feelings of your prospect, but not necessarily indicating your agreement. "I believe that I understand why you're upset with the college. If I have this right, you believe that they should have acknowledged your gift in a different way. . ."

Or another method I use is something such as: "That's really helpful input. Let's look at that in depth. I think that could be helpful to me." This is not yielding, only acknowledging.

The acknowledgment shows that you have listened and you understand the prospect's position. Your objective is not to beat the prospect, but to respond to the objection. Don't overlook the concern. Acknowledge it and respond in a positive way to the institution's position. It's what poet John Keats meant in *Negative Capability* when he spoke about a person who is confronted with facts counter to his dearly held truths: "You may not like it. You bow to the inevitable. You have to listen."

16　*Silent* is an analogue for *listen*. This isn't terribly significant but I find it rather symbolic. Here's the lesson: listening effectively and assertively is never passive. Your silence requires all of the mental agility and energy you can muster.

17　And finally, my *Magic 11 Minutes*.

Our research shows that you have a maximum of eleven minutes to sell your dream. You are with your prospect. The moment has come when you must talk of how important their investment will be in saving lives and changing lives. Your message is powerful, you are spinning your magic. But what we find is that anything beyond eleven minutes, and prospects' minds begin wandering. Their eyes glaze over. They are mentally *out to lunch*. All your fine words become a verbal Jacuzzi to your prospect.

The 11 minutes don't begin during the early stages of your visit. That's when you're building common ground and rapport. It starts when you begin the presentation of your vision, your dreams, and how this project will ultimately benefit the prospect. You talk about the joy. You talk about the lives that will be served and saved. You have eleven precious minutes to weave that magic—no more.

Prime Minister Cromwell, in a heated debate at Parliament, once said: "I beseech to you to think it possible you may be wrong." On this, I'm not wrong. Eleven minutes. No more.

FasTrack Tenets

1   Hearing is the science phase in receiving communications. Listening is the art. Become an artist.

2   When you talk instead of listen:

- You're not learning anything about the prospect.

- You will not hear any of their concerns.

- You will not uncover any giving-clues.

- You may raise negative issues.

- You do not allow the prospect to gain ownership.

- You dominate the conversation instead of guiding it.

- You don't give the prospect center stage.

- You don't give yourself breathing time to think ahead.

3   Prospects are more apt to respond to questions that you pose than to information that you give them. That's the sad truth of it, no matter how eloquent your presentation.

4   Studies show that the greater your ability to listen, the more likely the other person will listen to you. The more you talk, the less your prospect listens.

5   Give your undivided attention to the person. This sends a message that he or she is very special, respected, and valued.

6   When some think of communications, the first thought is *sending*. By far, the greatest percentage of our time and the most important is in *receiving*— listening.

7   The person asking the questions and probing is in control of the conversation. The only dumb question is the one you don't ask.

8   If you are in fundraising, you are in the listening business. Spend your time listening and observing.

9   Be concerned about the non-verbal signals. They tell a great deal about your prospect's true feelings and intentions—more than the words that he or she speaks.

10 You win the person to you by listening. It's not your eloquence or your charmed words. Listening does the trick.

11 Be certain your prospect is seated and comfortable. Be on the alert to any signals that might indicate that your prospect is becoming anxious or disinterested.

12 Most prospects won't really listen or pay attention to your presentation until they are absolutely convinced you have heard and appreciated their point of view. They want to be heard. The most effective way to make an impact is to have the prospect interpret his or her point of view before you present yours.

13 Learn how to find out if your prospect is really listening.

14 Work on your voice. Practice. Make certain there's inflection, variance of volume, changes in speed. Put zest into what you're saying.

15 Listening effectively and assertively is not passive. Your silence requires mental agility and all the energy you can muster.

16 After you have taken time to listen carefully, examine every possible facet, probe and ask proper questions—you have eleven minutes to make your presentation. Eleven minutes. No more!

PART II

THE MAGIC MIX

9
Money And Trustees

She was upset. Plenty upset. And when she finished, some folks were nodding in agreement.

"They promised me that I wouldn't have to raise money." I felt she could have kept her voice down just a bit. It was not a pleasant moment. "I told them that I'd come on the board, but I wouldn't call on anyone for a gift. And I told them that I wouldn't be able to make a gift myself."

And there were all those other board members concurring. It was obvious they were given the same promise when they were recruited.

I was thinking, what would Si Seymour have said in a situation like this. He would have had a wise retort, a perfect response. Oh, Si—where are you when I need you?

I looked at the chairman of the Board, and then the Headmaster. They gave me no comfort. The chair was staring off in space. The Headmaster's eyes were transfixed on a sheet of paper, head buried, I couldn't make eye contact.

Why the devil had they enlisted board members with the promise that giving and fundraising would not be a function of trusteeship—when this represented the school's most urgent need?

Yes, yes—I know. Trustees can bring qualities other than fundraising that are critical to the institution. The three **Ws** are still a valid paradigm: ***Work, Wisdom, and Wealth***. Add an additional *W*—***Wallop***. You want men and women of influence—Wallop. You seek all four *W*s in a trustee, and reverently hope for at least three of the *W*s.

If your institution does not have the financial resources to fulfill its mission (***Wealth***), no matter how heavily involved trustees are (***Work***), and no matter how wise they are in their decisions (***Wisdom***)—you will flag, falter, and fail. Your high ideals and promise will go unanswered and unresolved.

I hear it so often: *I give time and therefore I shouldn't be expected to give money*. But it's naive for a trustee to think that just giving time will provide the resources necessary to thrust the institution forward. Time alone will not transform a so-so organization into a good one, a good one into a great one. It takes money.

Particularly in today's world where the squeeze is tighter, the funds scarcer, and the budgets more constrained and constricted—the admonition: *Give, Get, or Get Off* is irrefutably relevant.

At the board meeting I referred to earlier, the school had discussed for years the need for new and added facilities. The school cannot maintain a quality program without the infusion of funds that comes from a larger student body. And this requires new facilities.

The board discusses the need for new facilities regularly. And has for years. The project is one of their great wishes. But that's all it is—a wish. And that's all it will ever be, a wish, until they have the level of trustees who have the capacity and the will to give.

On this board, there has never really been the resolve and the determination to make it happen. "Gee, I wish we could have more classrooms." That's as far as the board gets.

No resolve, no will, no funds. No classrooms!

I grant you, it's not easy being a trustee. Difficult times, these. The legal liabilities, new regulations, and fiduciary responsibilities never end. And there are the concerns about staff. All those objectives that are not reached. Deadlines that aren't met. And meetings, meetings, meetings. Too much to read, but not enough information. How can you make an informed decision?

At one college board meeting recently, a trustee said to me: "All we talk about at board meetings are the three Bs—budgets, buildings, and baloney!"

The future isn't what it used to be! *Carpe Diem* isn't good enough. Not in today's world. *Seize the Day* won't do it. For institutions and trustees, in order to keep pace, the credo must be: *Seize the Future*.

Too many trustees practice *analysis paralysis*. The parade will pass them by. Certainly there is the need to plan carefully. Of course. But instead of Ready, Aim, Aim, Aim, Aim . . . you will have to switch to Ready,

Fire, Aim. There's an expression attributed to Napoleon: "First charge, then let's see what happens." To win and be successful, today's trustee must have a thorough understanding of the future and a strong bias for action.

A Fail-Proof Check List

At times trustees do not perform as they should. Indeed, they may not be properly informed as to how significant it is for them to support, defend, publicize, and strengthen their institutions. Here are twelve criteria you can use to measure your board's performance. These twelve provide an invincible standard for trustee excellence.

1 **Mission is Everything.** Trustees work at understanding the institution, its history, and its present program and outreach. They understand that everything that is done by the institution, all new programs being planned, all its visions for the future—must be measured within the parameters of the institution's mission.

As board members, they are prudent stewards of the institution's resources. More than that, they make certain that the use of funds reflects the primary mission of the institution and its unique priorities.

Trustees understand that the mission is the organization's most prized treasure—to be taken out often for public display, to be cherished, and to be polished regularly to make certain it maintains its luster and value.

2   **Courage to Challenge.** Trustees must bring to each board meeting a probing, challenging, open mind. They must question the *status quo* and measure each new program and activity with a searing examination of whether the organization is meeting its mission. There must be dazzling dreams and glorious visions for the future, all wrapped around the mission. There is no time to loll or relax, or take the tranquilizing drug of gradualism. Things must be done now. Time will not wait.

3   **Faithful Attendance.** Trustees are conscientious about attending board and committee meetings. They participate fully, openly, and with candor.

They come well prepared for all board and committee meetings. This is especially true if they are asked to make decisions that have high impact on the future of the organization and those it serves. They never vote without proper understanding and preparation.

4   **Fervor and Institutional Zeal.** Trustees are thunder and thumping advocates on behalf of the institution. At every opportunity possible, they speak with enthusiasm and ardor about the organization.

Trustees can only do their most effective best and give to the fullest extent, both their leadership and dollars—to those organizations where they have deep conviction and raging enthusiasm. Trustees provide the greatest contribution possible when there is a love affair with their organization. A zeal. A passion.

That's it. Passion. A trustee with passion is a majority.

5   **Persuade Others.** Trustees bring to bear all of the influence possible to persuade others to act on behalf of the institution. They help get gifts from others—friends, colleagues, and neighbors. They are enthusiastic advocates, movers and doers.

I tell board members that once every day, they should talk to someone about the great work of their organization. (Not their spouse, at least not everyday!) I give them weekends off. That's five days a week. I even give them the summer off. That's only forty weeks a year. But that means 200 contacts a year. Just think of a roaring ripple effect. But that's just one board member. Multiply that times the number of members you have on your board.

6   **Excellence is Everything.** Trustees settle for nothing less than the best. They make certain that all activities and offerings are the highest quality possible. They understand that the institution's success is in direct proportion to the Board's commitment to excellence.

It is indeed a very strange phenomenon of trusteeship—when you are willing to accept mediocrity in staff work and programs, you will get mediocre work. Board members understand that they do not have the luxury of mediocrity.

7   **Good Business Judgment.** Trustees must bring their wisest business acumen and judgment into the boardroom. They decide what is the very best for the cause, and they fight for it. After the vote is taken,

they act as an adult—even if they were against the action. If they simply can't tolerate the decision and it becomes a matter near impossible to deal with, they give serious consideration to leaving the board. None of this snit nonsense!

And mixed heartily with their good judgment, trustees should bring compassion, sensitivity, and heart, combined with a strong business sense and a financial point of view.

What an organization really wants in a board member is a combination of the compassion of a Mother Theresa and the business sense of a Warren Buffett.

8   **Know the Competition.** Trustees develop a good understanding of the competition. They make certain that their organization is out front. They don't like to lose. They are winners. They understand that a good loser is a loser. The key to win-power is want-power. Board members must want their institution to be the best. Trustees who want something badly enough will find the win-power to achieve it.

The thrust must not necessarily be to get ahead of others—although this is indeed an important benchmark. What is important is to get ahead of ourselves, to break old records, outstrip our yesterdays by today. Hard work. To think the possible.

9   **Work Hard at the Job.** Trustees volunteer. When assignments come up, even those that are difficult and fairly time-consuming—they offer to take them on. At first, this shocks their fellow trustees. But after a short while, that kind of spirit catches on. It is contagious.

10 **Applause for the Staff.** Trustees provide accord and acclaim for good performance. Trustees have a right to expect the very best possible from staff and the chief executive officer. The truth is, however, that not every organization has a staff that comes up to this high expectation. When it does, trustees have a responsibility to let the staff know about it. It is amazing, the wondrous things that can be achieved when a staff receives its proper recognition. Even salary recognition!

11 **They Give.** Good trustees give sacrificially.

Ouch! You knew I was going to get to this. Trustees are expected to give to the very best of their abilities. No one ever tells them how much to give. But it is certainly expected that they do as much as they possibly can because they are a trustee. If trustees don't give, and don't give devotedly—why should anyone else? Albert Camus said: "And if you true believers don't help us, who else in the world can help us do this?"

12 **Concentrate Their Effort.** Trustees need to take a good look at their own volunteer workload. It is possible that they may not be able to serve on more than a few boards at one time.

It is hard to be a roaring advocate and a sacrificial giver to a large number of organizations. And it is difficult to give the kind of time that is necessary. Time and energy should be carefully rationed for those boards and institutions that trustees love the most.

One day, speaking to a gathering of thousands, Mahatma Gandhi warned his people of what he called *The Seven Sins of the World.*

He described these sins as: "Wealth without work. Pleasure without conscience. Knowledge without character. Commerce without morality. Science without humanity. Worship without sacrifice. Politics without principle."

I have a list to suggest, also, appropriate and relevant for board members—*The Seven Sins of Trusteeship.*

- Acceptance without commitment.

- Membership without attendance.

- Affiliation without dedication.

- Meetings without participation.

- Decisions without integrity.

- Involvement without advocacy.

- Association without giving.

Trustees and staff, working together, must have the will, the fortitude, and the resolution to dare. There must be a systematic pursual to plunge, to speculate, to inquire, to imagine, to doubt, to explore.

And trustees must encourage the staff in this regard. The greater the risk, the greater the reward. The institution that dares believes in the doctrine of the possible. To take the initiative—that's what counts. To accept the lead, to lust for the risk. There must be a willingness to attack the bold, arduous, seemingly impossible undertaking.

This will mark the truly effective board and successful organization.

Board members seek the explosive opportunity to take a chance and run with it. And win! There is no time to doubt. Trustees and the staff, joined in this courageous venture, make the impossible possible, and succeed where ordinary prudence fails.

But it's not always easy. And most often, it requires funds—new funds.

The institution that is willing to forge the unknown and place new ideas in confrontation with the old may be taking a leap of faith into new budget requirements. It requires trustees with a spirit that welcomes nonconformity, and yes—zeal, exuberance, and ardor for the unexplored. Breaking new barriers and seeking new frontiers. And no matter what the cost, the travel is worthy of the travail.

There are four levels of board members. Those who make things happen, those who watch things happening, those to which things happen, and those who don't even know what's happening. You want board members who make things happen. Eschew the others.

History will deal kindly with your institution if your trustees and staff have an abhorrence for everything that is dull, motionless, and unrisking. No rigidity. No timidity.

Trustees must give their heart, and their spirit, and their funds—to the terror, the surprise, the fear, and the exhilaration of the unexplored.

FASTRACK TENETS

1   Today's needs are unending, the challenges are un-yielding. The marketplace becomes more and more competitive. *Carpe Diem, Seize the Day*, is no longer relevant. Today it's: *Seize the Future.*

2   Mission is everything. Board members understand that all programs being planned and all visions for the future must be measured within the perimeters of the institution's mission.

3   Director's have the courage to challenge, to explore new ventures, attempt the unthinkable. *Status quo* is repugnant.

4   Faithful attendance is a priority. Directors must be roaring advocates on behalf of the institution. There must be passion. It must be like fire in their bones.

5   Board members must influence others on behalf of the organization.

6   Excellence is everything. Board members must not settle for anything less than the very best.

7   A good board member understands the competition. They make certain that the organization is out-front, ahead of the field.

8   There is applause for the staff. Trustees provide recognition for good performance.

9   Because it requires time, energy, money, and dedication—trustees limit the number of boards they serve on.

10

Go On To The Next One

He shook his finger at me. It was obvious that this was a topic he felt keenly about.

"I'd go on to the next one. That's what I'd do." That is C. Allen Favrot speaking. And Allen knows what he's talking about. He is a great community leader, a volunteer of monumental proportions.

And when Allen Favrot speaks, you better listen! He has striking credentials. He has been chair and chief volunteer officer of the United Way in New Orleans, and chair of the board of directors of the YMCA. He has headed both the United Way campaign and several capital campaigns for the YMCA. He has been the driving force behind every effort in New Orleans that serves the social and human agenda of that community. He has accrued dozens of citations, honors, and leadership roles.

What prompted Allen's comment was when I asked him the other day what his reaction would be if he spoke to a person about serving on a board and the man or woman said: "I'll join the board, but you can't count on me for a gift and I won't call on anyone."

"Allen," I asked, "what would you do?"

"I'd go on to the next one. I wouldn't consider adding someone to one of the boards I serve on who isn't interested enough to make a gift or willing to call on others for a donation. I don't care how well known he is in the community or what his name might mean to the organization. It would be obvious that he doesn't bring the kind of commitment that is necessary. I'd pass him by and go on to the next one.

"Give, get, or get off. I really practice that. If you don't get someone who is willing to work and give, you are settling for less than the best. And I don't think any institution can afford that these days."

Allen is right. An organization cannot afford to have board members who aren't pulling their weight. That's because, more than ever before, organizations face an insatiable appetite for funds. It won't get better. Having the right board can make the difference.

There is no question about it—proper funding, if appropriately used, can secure and keep quality staff. It can buy necessary equipment and build the facilities you need. Money provides scholarships, important scientific research, support for youth activities, service for the elderly, and an unending array of essential activities and programs.

Your organization has an unequaled and invincible mission. The need for your service is undeniable and its justification for support is dramatic and emotionally captivating. If presented properly, the case and cause are irresistible. If it isn't all of this, you may be in trouble. If you don't fit a very special niche—be forewarned: in today's competitive marketplace, you may be *niched* by another organization that's gaining on you.

Having proper financial support is essential. Having adequate funding is the difference between being on the runway and actually taking off. You want to fly.

Over the years, I judge I have worked professionally with over 2000 organizations across the country and around the world. I've been the chief executive officer of two nonprofits, mother and father to 400 YMCAs on the East Coast, a member of eight nonprofit boards, and vice president of a college. So much for my credentials!

I've seen institutional life from every side of the table. I believe I know something about nonprofit structure and work. I am convinced that the success, outreach, and mission-achievement of an institution is in direct proportion to the commitment and dedication of its board.

The trouble is, most organizations and most staffs spend precious little time and consideration in what should be a matter of priority significance—enlisting the most effective board possible.

Now, don't get huffy! I'm certain I'm correct on this. You're guilty as charged! Think for a moment that your organization is a bit like this group I'm going to describe.

I met recently with 53 men and women who are chief executive officers of the Easter Seal Society. These are the professionals who head the largest Easter Seal Chapters in the country. They are great people—bright, effective, and eager to succeed. I was talking to them about how they spend their time.

Much of this won't surprise you. Most of their time is spent in administration. Next comes meetings—with staff and volunteers. All kinds of meetings. Meetings, meetings, meetings. For some, it amounts to as much as 50 percent of their time. One executive told me that these meetings bring together "a collection of individuals who separately do nothing and together decide that nothing can be done. The unfit trying to lead the unwilling to do the unnecessary!"

Virtually all spend 2 percent of their time, or less, on trustee recruitment and development. Two percent or less!

If it is true, and it is, that the board of an organization determines and assures the program and services, the funding, and the validity and vitality of the institution—you need the strongest board possible. If it is true, and again it is, that the board defines and charts the destiny of your organization, you need the most effective and devoted directors possible. That's why it is difficult to understand why so little time is given to such a consequential imperative. It's the life of your organization we're talking about.

It is not enough for nonprofit chief executive officers to do things right. They must do the right things. And most significant among these right things is having a Board that is vital, active, and dedicated. You want a Board that holds the institution to unsparing standards of performance.

The most effective executives I have worked with are Money Tree-shakers and trustee-makers. The most successful among these executives spend appropriate time on board development—present and future. And it pays.

The character and strength of the institution's board is almost always in direct proportion to the strategy and amount of time that is given to enlistment and training. And in this, the staff shares a major and inescapable responsibility.

Eight Irrefutable Principles

Here are eight axioms which influence the character and practice of the nonprofit board:

1   You will find it easier to recruit and keep good board members for your organization if you have a successful operation. No one wants to serve and give time to help save the sinking Titanic.

2   Strong board members are attracted to strong staff. The more effective the chief, the more effective the board. The chief executive officer helps define and determine the type of person who chooses to serve on the board. If you have a weak chief, chances are that you will have a weak board.

3   Fundraising cannot be conducted successfully without board members who are influential, affluential, and affirmative.

4   Excellence in the institution doesn't just happen. It requires a shared commitment on the part of both staff and board to be nothing less than the best. Together, they keep raising the bar. It's interesting to

note that with the organizations I have worked with—if the board and chief officer are willing to accept anything less than excellence, that's what they get.

5   A board that is unwilling to pay effective and productive staff appropriate salaries often gets the kind of staff it deserves.

6   Board members who do not prepare properly for board meetings often make poor decisions. They should never complain about the organization's focus or direction. Their inattention sets the course for a rudderless journey in stormy waters. No compass, no direction, no bearings, no leader. No future.

7   A whole world of capable men and women is waiting to be asked to serve on your board. I am convinced of it. They are magnificent people and will contribute mightily in every way to your work. They are just waiting to be asked. Here is a rule you can consider gospel: *You will be hurt more by those who were not asked and would have said yes—than by those who say no.*

8   Board members will keep surprising you. They are forged, not easily found. But they'll stand on tiptoes for the right mission, the right program and the right staff. They'll take on assignments that they would once have never considered. They are often quite ordinary men and women, willing to make extraordinary commitments.

Here's What Board Members Must Do

From time to time, I'm asked at a board meeting what I consider to be the major criteria of a trustee. There are those who wish they hadn't asked! As a consultant, I have discovered that board members are allowed to ask questions, but are not always obliged to listen!

1   An effective board member must understand the institution, its history, its present program, and its outreach. A trustee must be dedicated to the mission and measure everything the organization does in relation to its philosophy of operation.

Understanding the purpose of the organization means that the board member knows the distinctiveness of the mission, what sets you apart. They realize that you cannot market if you do not have a clear and focused vision. This means being aware of those with a similar service.

2   A board member must be faithful about attending board and committee meetings—and participate fully, openly, and with candor. I consider 70% attendance to be a minimum level. Anything below that is unacceptable. (A number of foundations now will not consider a grant if your attendance is less than 70%.)

3   In today's world, there is little tolerance for delay, dawdling, and diddling. This means expediting the decision making process; the vagaries of the marketplace forces a strategic sensitivity to time. Decisions need to be driven by the **2-Ms**: **Market** and **Mission**—backed up by data. In today's world, off-the-

cuff determinations will not suffice. It often requires market research, cost analysis, penetrating and effective analysis. In today's world, putting off a decision is actually making a decision—and you may not like the outcome.

4   A board member must be a roaring advocate. At every opportunity possible, a director speaks with enthusiasm and an unquestionable ardor about the organization.

5   He or she brings to bear all the influence possible to persuade others to act in a positive way on behalf of the organization.

6   *Alchemy* means the transmutation of base metal into gold. Robertson Davies, the great Canadian author, says what alchemy really means is something that has attained such excellence, such nearness to perfection, that it "offers a glory, and the expansion of life and understanding, to those who have been brought in contact with it." That's what board members are—the alchemists.

7   New ideas in motion. That's what will thrust your organization forward. Board members need to be challenged to embrace new ideas as conditions change and need to be changed. If trustees are properly prepared, and the situation is properly interpreted, they will move faster than you ever thought possible. They need to continually rethink the institution's mission and business. Your competitors already are. They need the gift of prophecy. They understand that what is good enough today is unacceptable tomorrow.

8   A trustee settles for nothing less than the best. He or she understands that the difference between big and great . . . is very small. A trustee makes certain that all activities and offerings of the institution are of the highest quality possible. And a board member understands that when you refuse to accept anything but the very best, you most often get the best. To a world filled with compromise and mediocrity, they make no contribution.

9   A board member brings his or her business acumen into the boardroom. And is intrepid about making tough decisions. They ask the *what* and *why* questions—not the how questions.

10 They volunteer, that's what good trustees do. There are assignments that come up, some that are difficult and fairly time-consuming. A dedicated board member takes them on. I tell them that at first, they may shock fellow trustees with their willingness. But after a short while, that kind of spirit catches on. It is contagious. Success happens only with dedication and hard work.

11 Many don't like this next part. I tell them what some don't like to hear. But it's okay—they expected me to say it. And I remind them that they asked me. They must give sacrificially. That means that they give to the very best of their ability. They stretch. And, they help get gifts from others—friends, business associates, neighbors. I tell them that at first, these friends and colleagues may be tempted to duck you—but your enthusiasm will be so infectious they will find the cause irresistible.

12   Board members provide accord and acclaim for the
     good work of the staff. A board has the responsibil-
     ity to expect the very best performance possible
     from the staff. The truth is, not every organization
     has a staff that comes up to this high expectation.
     When it does, the board must applaud and give sup-
     port. And I tell them: "If you have a really effective
     staff, in order to recognize and hold them—try chok-
     ing them with gold!"

Recently, I completed a manuscript on trusteeship.
In the course of preparing the material, I interviewed
about 100 men and women who serve on boards. These
were wonderful, caring people. One of the most notable
was Winton M. Blount.

Everyone knows him as *Red*. He told me: "I like it
when people call me Red. It reminds me of when I still
had hair!"

Red Blount is one of the largest donors and one of
the major leaders of all good causes in Montgomery, Al-
abama. He has been involved as an active volunteer and a
generous donor for dozens of organizations, for years and
years. He understands that being a giver and a volunteer
is reaching your fullest potential as a human being. Much
of the vitality and strength and direction of major nonprofits in Montgomery is attributable to Blount's commitment and devotion. He told me something that was
fascinating.

"Whenever I give time and money to one of my organizations," Blount said, "I always get it back. The more
time I volunteer and the more money I give, the better I

seem to do personally. There's no rationale or explanation for this—it just happens."

I heard virtually the same type of comment from every single one of the Board members I interviewed for my study. What they give, they get back. And they get it back many times over. One board member told me: "Life is a wheel. It goes round and round. And the more I give, the more that comes back to me."

Ahh, the altruism concept is alive and well.

No other activity can match the dimension and breadth of trusteeship. All the board members I spoke with felt they were part of something truly significant and that their involvement was worth all the time and energy they gave. There wasn't even time to ask: "Who the devil talked me into this in the first place?"

I've worked with all kinds of board members. There are those I call the well-poisoners. These are the doom-sayers. They are the ones who will tell you why things won't work out, that it's been tried before, and it can't be done. They are against just about everything. And ring their hands in despair. Life is drudgery and a bore. They pass it on to the organization.

Then there are the institutional-maintainers. These are the directors who insist that things be kept as they are. They are adamant for steadfast stagnation. They yearn for the good old days and cherish the *status quo*. These trustees take care of things, they maintain, and they make certain that everything is quite tidy. They never step out of their box.

And then there are those special ones, the institutional-enrichers. Let's recite psalms. These are the men and women who at every opportunity possible find a new way to renew and revitalize the institution.

If properly challenged, the institutional-enrichers will achieve glorious objectives for your organization. They'll reach new horizons for you. You will soar.

Board members will not disappoint you, not if they understand and experience the joy of being head-over-heels involved in your work. It is one of the glorious celebrations of this life that no one can help another without helping him or herself. Having the right board members will, in the end, help your institution resonate with service and overflow with activities. The proper board sustains your mission and ensures your future.

Your board members just need to be reminded that their major responsibility is to make certain that your organization has the proper funding. Money makes it happen.

Be one with Allen Favrot. If you can't count on the dedication and commitment of a prospective or present board member, go on to the next one.

FasTrack tenets

1   Board members must give and they must ask others to give. *Give, get, or get off* is a principle that should be followed.

2   Proper funding can secure and keep quality staff, and buy necessary equipment and build facilities. Having the right board can make all of that happen.

3   You get the kind of board you deserve. If you do not have a structured and organized process for recruiting *the right* board members, you will end up with less than effective trustees.

4   Strong board members are attracted to successful organizations. They are attracted to staff people who are dynamic and effective.

5   Fundraising cannot be conducted successfully without board members who are influential, affluential, and affirmative.

6   Excellence in an institution requires the strong commitment of both the staff and volunteers to high aspirations and objectives. Board members should be willing to pay appropriate salaries for staff people who are effective and productive.

7   Board members who do not prepare properly for board meetings very often make poor decisions.

8   There is a whole world waiting to be asked to serve on your board. They just need to be asked. Aim high. You will be hurt more by those who are not asked and would have said *yes*—than by those who say *no*.

9 Trustees should fully understand the history, program, and outreach of their institution.

10 Anything less than seventy percent attendance should be considered unacceptable.

11 A board member should settle for nothing less than the very best in its staff, its programs, and services.

11

Lunch With Sandy   ·

I'm having lunch the other day, at the Four Seasons in New York, with my good friend Sandy Weil. Sanford I. Weil is Chairman and Chief Executive Officer of the Travelers Group, and the largest stockholder. They just acquired Salomon Brothers for $9 billion.

We lunch at the Four Seasons fairly often and they always reserve a very special table for Sandy. It's always a great treat for me. Because he's such a regular there at lunch time, he's one of the few they allow to smoke a cigar in the restaurant.

We exchange the usual pleasantries.

> "How's Joan?" I ask.
> "Great," he says. "How's Felicity?"
> "Great, never better."

I want to get down to the business of fundraising. That's what our luncheon is supposed to be about. Sandy Weil has been Chair of The Carnegie Hall since 1991, when he took over from James Wolfensohn, President of the World Bank. It's quite a story.

Before we start our discussion about Carnegie Hall, I ask him the question that is on everyone's mind—how he finally put the deal together to acquire Salomon Brothers. It seemed so improbable.

(He tells me about another acquisition that's about to break, a real blockbuster. But he swears me to secrecy.)

"Well as a matter of fact," Sandy says, "it all began following a Carnegie Hall board meeting. Deryck (Deryck Maughan, Chairman of Salomon Brothers) pulled me aside. 'You know the subject we talk about every now and then?' Deryck says. 'Now may be the appropriate time to have that conversation about the future of our companies.' "

The Carnegie board is one of the most prestigious in the country. Trustees rub elbows with fellow titans and there are plenty of deals that are launched right at the board table. It's just one of the features that makes a seat on this board one of the hottest in the country.

It's an elite group with sixty-five coveted slots. It's so prestigious that even top corporate executives eagerly audition for subcommittees just to win a chance with the big group. "It wasn't always that way," Sandy says. He takes immense pride in the board, which is considered one of the toughest in New York to get on.

For years, Carnegie Hall was floundering, near bankruptcy. So bad were its finances, the beautiful landmark building was scheduled to be torn down to make way for an office tower. It was saved only after virtuoso Violinist Isaac Stern helped persuade political and social leaders to save the Hall. It was purchased by New York City and spared the wrecking ball. But that's a whole other story for another time.

"Back then," Sandy says, "the board had perfectly nice people, but no money. Musicians, but no muscle. It wasn't a chic place to belong. No social cachet.

"When I became chairman, I saw the board slots as a way to flatter financial heavy weights, and then tap into their personal and corporate bank accounts. The change in the board started when we decided we needed to raise serious money.

"What's interesting is that the tougher we seem to make it to get on our board—the more top leaders clamor for election. I think there's an important lesson in that. In order to have a really strong board, you need to make it clear that not everyone is eligible for membership. There's a cost—in terms of giving and getting."

I ask him how tough is it to get on the board. "Plenty! We have an exacting process for picking new members. And as I said, because it is so difficult, it seems to make it even more attractive to belong. And I can tell you, anyone who tries to orchestrate his own nomination will probably not be asked. If you have to lobby, you aren't going to make it."

We finish the appetizers and are into our entrée by now. Sandy goes on to explain. "First and foremost, each candidate is evaluated for financial heft. The truth is, we look at what a person is worth, what he gives to other organizations, and how he spends his money in general. We look at real estate records, income sources, stockholdings, and Securities and Exchange commission filings. We look at everything.

"We want to know what kind of gifts he has made to his college and to hospitals, and what other boards he serves on. We even examine his charitable giving compared with his personal spending and how hard he works when he serves on a board.

"Listen, selecting the right board members is the most important decision you can make. The board is your future. It determines the kind of financial base you are going to have and how effectively you will meet your mission. It is everything. It is your destiny. With the right board, you can do anything.

"When we meet with potential board candidates, we have all of this good research and background information. If their projected giving doesn't meet what we think they can give—well, that doesn't show a good enough commitment. They probably won't make it."

Sandy goes on to explain that candidates must also demonstrate a willingness to commit their time. He considers that very important. "You've heard about the young woman who asked the policeman how to get to Carnegie Hall. 'Practice, practice, practice.' Well, that's what typically happens with candidates. First they serve on an advisory committee or a subcommittee for a few years. If they do a good job and show the proper commitment, both in time and giving, they stand a chance of making the first string.

"Let me tell you about Craig Weatherup (CEO of PepsiCo)," Sandy says. "We had him working as the Co-Chair of the corporate committee for three years—to see if he could beef up corporate sponsorships. We watched him carefully. He did a great job and earned his stripes. We elected him a couple of years ago to serve on the board. That's pretty typical."

There's another test. Board prospects have to really love music and attend Carnegie Hall concerts. "If they're not interested in music, they shouldn't be on the board." says Sandy.

Sandy then tells me about Ruddi Stalder (head of private banking at Credit Suisse). There were a number of meetings and luncheons he attended before Stalder was actually invited to serve on the board. During that time, Stalder attended twenty concerts. "We don't spy, but we are able to check ticket sales. If they're buying tickets, we assume they're not sending the maid. A passion for the place is really important to us."

The final *gut-check* for a prospective director is what Sandy calls the *Compatibility Test*. "Carnegie makes a lot of demands on its directors. In the end, you really have to enjoy being together as a group. I want it to be a nice, friendly club where we're partners and social friends at the same time. I love warm and fuzzy."

The nominees who do make it recognize they have attained something quite special. They dive into their board work, while savoring and networking the perks.

We order dessert. "The big pay-off is financial. We're not coy about the requirement that every director be totally engaged, though it can be a bit expensive. For starters, they are expected to give $10,000 to $100,000 a year to the annual fund." Sandy tells me that they understand that they are to give to the endowment fund and other special projects, also. The average director's personal gift to the endowment fund is $600,000.

"We want them to use their great contacts to solicit big gifts from others. It comes with the territory. If you're on the board of a nonprofit, you are supposed to use your contacts. You're expected to call on others for gifts. That's a given.

"We count on their expertise, too. Some have technology contacts that are important to us. We have the Vice Chairman of Chase Manhattan Bank to advise us on our finances. We have the top attorney in the country to help us with legal matters."

Sandy lights one of those big cigars he's become famous for. He offers me one. Heck, I light up, too. Then he tells me about the great Isaac Stern, who serves as the Hall's *musical conscience*. "When Stern is at a board meeting, he always speaks at the end and without a prepared text. He inspires us, and reminds us of what Carnegie is all about. We leave there excited, enthusiastic, and with a sense of mission."

A couple of corporate-types stop by our table. Sandy introduces me. They talk about a performance they attended a couple weeks ago, and they are glowing. (Maybe they are board-hopefuls, I think, trying to make an impression.) It is obvious to me that they are just as starry-eyed about being in the presence of Sandy Weil as having been in the splendor of Carnegie Hall.

And now, dear reader, a confession. (It's good for the soul.) I don't know Sanford Weil and I haven't been at the Four Seasons in three or four years. The luncheon and the discussion did not take place.

Wait a minute. Don't be upset. All of the comments and the quotes are true. Let me explain.

There was a wonderful article in a recent *Wall Street Journal* about Carnegie Hall and Mr. Weil's role in building the Board. There were some quotes, and I used them selectively in this chapter. I didn't change the meaning or the thrust of anything. In addition to the *WSJ* article, I heard Mr. Weil speak on one occasion about *his* board and the great pride he has in it. I added some of that. What I have written is faithful with all that guides him.

I used this format because I thought it was interesting. And fun. But I don't want you to miss what I consider to be eight basic and significant truths, great lessons that should guide you in your thinking regarding the board and its membership.

1   **THE BOARD IS YOUR FUTURE.** There's nothing of greater significance to the future of your Institution than the quality of your board. Directors are expected to bring what I refer to as the *Four Ws*: work, wealth, wisdom, and wallop! Your board isn't something that is important. It is everything. With the right board, you have an exciting tryst with destiny.

2   **SIZE ISN'T IMPORTANT.** I hear it all the time: "We need a small board so we can be effective in making important decisions. If you have too large a group, you never decide on anything."

Well . . . the truth is, there really isn't that much to decide on at most board meetings. And not that often. It's not like you're making organization-shattering, institution-changing, structure-smashing decisions at every meeting. I find a large board is able to handle determinations effectively through small committees and careful preparation.

In the case of Carnegie Hall, they have sixty-five directors who are deeply and vitally engaged in the business of getting and giving. Personally, I prefer working with a large board. Here's why: I consider the most important function of a board the hiring of the Chief Executive Officer and their on-going evaluation. Next to that, and very close to in importance—I feel it is the board's responsibility to make certain that the organization does not run a "mission deficit." They need to ensure that there are sufficient funds to meet the institution's mission. That is a covenant they make, a commitment they cannot abdicate. And that means giving and getting. The more men and women you have involved in that, the better I like it.

3   **BE SELECTIVE**. Aim high. Don't settle for second best. Many organizations get the board members they *deserve*—rather than the board members they should have. By that I mean: those organizations that are casual, aimless, and unconstrained in recruiting—get the kind of board they deserve. Those that take their recruiting seriously, and make it an ongoing, structured, and highly refined process—enlist the kind of board that can propel an organization to towering heights.

It's all right to make it a little difficult to serve on your board. If you make it too easy to join, people don't feel that they are signing on to anything significant. It was Groucho Marx who said: "I would never belong to a club that would have me as a member." The same goes for your board membership.

I'm in favor of having board members sign a contract (a Letter of Understanding) that clearly outlines their responsibilities. That can be tough. It puts it on the line unmistakably what their charge is. And it provides unquestionable guidelines of what the organization must do for the board member. With this kind of a document, no one can misunderstand his or her role.

No matter how keen they are about your mission, and your service, your board members enjoy being part of a group that includes high-flying business and corporate types, people of prominence, influentials, and the social select. And they want to be a part of a board that includes their own level and circle of friends, or one class higher than theirs. I know how that sounds, but that's the truth of it.

Enlist men and women who focus on the future, who seek new trails, and are willing to break out of the past. You want those who live their lives and thrive on the adventure of tomorrow's great promise, who encourage the staff to develop finely honed skills, attitudes, and habits of mind, and all the dimensions of knowledge and understanding that will lead to continual change and renewal.

Select board members with entrepreneurial high-spirit. They will help you move your organization into the fast-changing lanes of the market fray. They will help you find and sell new products and services.

Choose board members who are willing to study and know the competition and the challenging environment. You'll need them to help dramatize and take advantage of your distinct mission.

Covet men and women who can drive and propel your organization's decision-making process. You need board members who understand the sense of urgency in today's market-driven roller coaster. Decisions have to be time-accelerated and strategically focused.

And be unafraid of the risk-takers. It can be a frightening and breathless mountain climb at times—but consider yourself richly blessed. They will lead you to new peaks you never thought you could reach. They will shatter the encrusted *status quo*, and help you cross a dazzling threshold of service and impact.

4   **THEY HAVE TO GIVE.** In today's world, it is unacceptable and unthinkable to have board members who do not give. How can you ask others to give if the board doesn't?

I called on the Community Foundation in Mansfield, Ohio, the other day on behalf of a client. The assets of the Foundation are small and their giving commensurate. Still, they are a significant force in this small community. Pamela, the Executive Director, told me that they would decide what to give to the organization when she saw what the board members were giving. "If they don't give what we feel they ought to, if they don't show their commitment—we'll pretty much match that lack of interest!" We find this same attitude around the country.

5   **THEY MUST ASK OTHERS TO GIVE.** I don't
find many board members queuing for the opportunity to call on prospects for a gift. James Gamble
(Proctor & Gamble and long-time Pasadena, California, board member of many organizations) is an
exception. 'That's my responsibility as a board
member and I just do it. Period!" At the very least,
directors should be door-openers for you, the kind
who will make appointments and go with a staff person on the call. They don't even have to say anything—just opening the door and arranging the visit
is important enough.

6   **THEY PROVIDE EXPERTISE.** Hopefully, in addition to all else they bring, recruit board members
who have special expertise and talents—the attorney
for legal issues, the banker for finances, the computer genius for your data processing, and that sort
of thing.

But avoid any semblence of conflict of interest. I
was with an organization the other day where a
board member told me he sold them all of their insurance. I would have disqualified him from being a
board member. You must give generously of your
talents and expertise to serve on a board, or you sell
your product (at the best price and service possible).
You don't do both.

7   **THEY GIVE TIME.** Unlike Stendhal's hero, who
thought he took part in something confused, disar-
rayed, and insignificant, that he later found out was
the Battle of Waterloo—good board members don't
watch from the sidelines. They get into the fray. It
means giving time. They volunteer when there are

jobs to be done and committees to serve on. And I find that the more time they give, the stronger and deeper their commitment to the institution grows.

It is assumed in all this that a director's attendance at board meetings is as close to perfect as possible. I called on a Dallas Foundation several months ago and presented a proposal. They liked the proposal, and then told me that all I needed to add was the board's attendance for the past eighteen months. I asked why. "If you don't have a minimum of 75% attendance, you don't even have to bother applying for a grant." At first blush, I thought this was severe. But think about it: why should a foundation give to your institution if the board doesn't care enough to attend meetings?

8   **BOARD MEMBERS NEED TO FEEL KEENLY ABOUT THE INSTITUTION.** There needs to be a commitment to your mission. More than that, you want board members who are burning in their bones for the organization. You want board members who are passionate for your work. Ahh, that's it. Passion! A board member who brings passion is the difference between an institution that flies and one that just flaps its wings. You want your organization to fly!

Have I told you about the lunch I had the other day with my good friend Bill Gates? Bill and I have lunch on a pretty regular basis. But that's a different story for another time.

FasTrack tenets

1   The board is your future, your destiny. Board members are expected to bring to their membership the Four **Ws**: **Work**, **Wealth**, **Wisdom**, and **Wallop**.

2   The size of the board isn't important. What is important is the size of their commitment.

3   The board must make certain that it does not run a *mission deficit.*

4   Be selective in choosing board members. Many organizations get the board members they deserve rather than the directors they should have. Aim high.

5   Have board members sign a letter of agreement, co-signed by the organization's chair and chief executive officer.

6   Enlist men and women who focus on the future, who are willing to abandon the *status quo* and burst out of the box.

7   Select those with entrepreneurial high-spirit. Be unafraid of the risk-takers.

8   Board members must give to their organization. If they don't, why should anyone else?

9   Board members have a responsibility to ask others to give.

10   Directors provide expertise to the organization.

11   Board members give time, energy, and talent.

12   Board members must bring a deep commitment to the mission of their organization.

12

Couldn't You Hear Me Keeping Quiet

I was thinking the other day about Harold Gores. I used to call on him regularly. At the time, he was President of the Educational Facilities Laboratories. This was a fascinating grant-giving group funded by the Ford Foundation. Its mission was to initiate innovative planning on college and high school campuses. New thoughts, new twists, new ways of doing things. Abandon the old, look for the new.

I was seeking a grant (and we finally got it) for my college-client. But my secondary reason for seeing Harold so regularly was that he was an absolutely delightful person, and one of the most visionary I have ever known. A session with him, and you'll feel like Emily Dickinson, "with the top of your head spinning off."

Before going to Educational Facilities Laboratories, Dr. Harold Gores was superintendent of the Newton, Massachusetts Schools. It was considered one of the most outstanding and innovative school systems in the country. I remember a fascinating story about Gores and his assistant superintendent, Joseph Carroll.

There was a meeting of the Board of Education. Harold Gores was there, of course, along with Carroll and other assistant superintendents. The board was having an agonizing time grappling with a problem. The board went round and round. The discussion became heated. There was confusion.

Joseph Carroll found it difficult to keep quiet. Finally, he found it impossible.

An assistant superintendent did not often speak up at a board meeting when not called upon. But Carroll stood up and suggested his approach for the board's consideration. The board members cheerfully embraced Carroll's suggestion as their own. The issue was quickly settled. On the spot.

Well, Carroll felt ten feet tall. Later, there was a midnight post-mortum held by Gores with his staff. Carroll prepared himself for the accolades he felt sure were coming his way. What he received instead was a lesson.

Gores said to him: "There's a time for helping the board find a solution, Joe. That's important. And there's a time for letting the board feel its own way and make its own decisions. A good administrator must learn the difference. In that discussion where you made the suggestion—*couldn't you hear me keeping quiet?*"

There is a great lesson in that, and Gores was always the master teacher. The best thing a chief executive officer can do for a board is to allow its members to discover their own soul and pace.

Boards and committees are now such a major part of our institutional life, we tend to take them for granted. I remind you that the first committee we know of that has been recorded is the one that was held for the Pennsylvania Hospital in Philadelphia. And the record shows that no one came to the meeting. Not even the chair. That was very likely a better meeting than some of you have attended.

I came across a piece the other day I had completely forgotten about. I had put it away years ago figuring I would use it sometime. You know how it is when you have something you want to keep and you don't know where to put it? (Do you have a better system than I do?) Well, I was rummaging through some old files, and there it was.

The piece is called the *Ten Commandments*. It's not exactly what you're thinking. I don't know who wrote the piece or came up with the idea. There's no name or identification on the material.

I've added an introduction, and changed the material—but not enough to call it my own. I've included it here because I have dealt so emphatically on the role of the board in the prior few chapters. It has a lot to say about today's board and committee structure.

The Ten Commandments

And many times, and for long hours, the multitudes gathered, seeking profound wisdom and guidance. But confusion reigned. Oft times, they were delayed in starting, late in ending. And verily I tell you, as the hours sped, the wisdom fled. It is recorded that the more often the people met, the less they accomplished.

The needs were great, but the ways were hidden. Those who were called multiplied, and the number of times they gathered increased.

Then from many came voices crying out, "Though I labor from the coming in to the going out, I cannot attend all the meetings for which I am summoned."

"The matter concerned me not, yet was I called into another meeting."

"The need for any decision is great, yet I am denied—for the leader listens not."

"To the meeting for which I made ready, no person came."

"Is thy servant a fool, that they summon him to a meeting to schedule yet another meeting?"

And then at last the chief, old and wise, hearing of these things decreed that an ax be laid to the root of those meetings which brought forth such bad fruits. And there was prepared a Tablet which contained great wisdom:

I   Thou shalt not meet if the matter can be resolved by other means.

II Thou shalt make the purpose of each meeting known to those thou summon.

III Thou shalt bring together only those whose presence is needful.

IV Thou shalt start at the time announced, and stop when it is neat and right so to do.

V   Thou shalt not run beyond.

VI   Thou shouldst combine into one meeting those which need not be separated.

VII   Prepare thy thoughts before thou speak, that the time of others be not wasted.

VIII   Schedule not in haste, for the day is short in which to do that which thou hast to do.

IX   Prepare not to meet or to cancel if there be no need.

And in time, the people learned and obeyed these writings. They followed them, putting to and taking away as suited their needs. As they forsook their old ways, new hours untold were given unto them. They were free to do great and important things. They saw that it was good.

And the Tenth Commandment? One who was very wise in years and knowledge proclaimed to all: "Cancel the meeting and save the donuts."

PART III

PERSONAL VICTORIES— LOSERS WEEPERS

13

Do What Your Mother Tells You

This is the saga of two real-life situations. One will send chills and uncontrollable quivering throughout your fundraising body. The other is the most extraordinary story you will ever hear.

Both happened within recent months. Both stories are truc. I've added a third—because it's so special.

Fasten your seatbelt.

In the first situation, I can't mention the name of the organization. You'll understand why in a moment. It is one of the nation's largest and most significant nonprofits.

The national office of the first organization I write about received a check for $20,000. It came from an acquisition mailing, from a woman they did not know. That size of a gift, in response to a form letter, is quite extraordinary. The fact that it came from an acquisition mailing, from someone who was not known, makes the gift all the more wondrous. But wait. This is only the beginning of the tale.

The organization's top fundraiser was quick to single out the $20,000 gift. Who wouldn't! She marked it for priority attention. She called the proper staff person and asked that an appropriate acknowledgment be made immediately. The nature and size of the gift called for more than just a letter and a receipt—certainly a phone call and more likely, a personal visit. This had the makings of something really intriguing, what John Steinbeck called, "blinding expectations."

Eight days after receiving the check, the organization received a call from the donor's attorney. Get ready for what happens next. The attorney reported that the donor had stopped payment on the check.

That's right! She rescinded the gift.

Here's what the attorney told the organization: "My client decided to make a gift of $20,000 to each of four national organizations. Her intention was to follow that with a truly significant gift to one of the four. But first, she wanted to see how quickly the organizations would respond. And she was curious what kind of a reply and acknowledgment she would receive. Which organization, she wondered, would be sufficiently grateful for the gift to be prompt in its acknowledgment and grateful in its spirit."

It turns out that one of the organizations responded immediately. There was a phone call the day they received the check and a personal visit three days later. Two of the organizations took a bit more time, but only by a day or two.

The organization I write about never even made it to the party. It turns out the person who was asked to follow-through on acknowledging the gift was too involved in other activities, including a special event. "I thought I would have a little more time. I had so many other important things I was doing," she said. "I didn't know there was that kind of a hurry about acknowledging it."

Now I'll tell you about another organization. This story has a happy ending. Well . . . more than that—a miraculous ending. You'll find it hard to believe. But it really happened. If you had been at the press announcement, in La Jolla, California, you could have heard about it first-hand.

But first, let me go back a few years.

For some time now, we have been telling clients that no matter how large and successful their fundraising machine, a gift of $1000 should be acknowledged with a personal telephone call. In fact, we began suggesting that a second call, from the support staff, was even in order where it seemed appropriate. "I'm calling, Mrs. Donor, because I'm just typing your receipt and getting ready to mail it. I noticed that this is the sixth year you have been a donor to our program. I just wanted you to know how very much your gift means to all of us. It is so very special to have you share in our work. All of us here are so grateful." I'm not certain why, but we find that kind of a call pays immense dividends—at times, more significant than a call from a professional or from the chief executive officer, where it might be more expected.

But something happened several years ago that made me change my thinking regarding the concept of the $1000 phone call.

At one of my seminars, I mentioned my rule about a telephone call for gifts of $1000 or more. After our session, one of the folks in attendance came up to the podium. She said: "I didn't want to interrupt, but I do want you to know that at St. Jude's (Memphis, Tennessee), we call everyone who gives $100 or more."

I was incredulous. "You're kidding. That's a heck of a lot of phone calls."

"It is. It's 44,000 calls a year."

I asked if it was worth it. And then quickly said: "You don't have to answer that. Of course it's worthwhile. You wouldn't be doing it otherwise."

And so I started telling my clients, and to anyone else who would listen, about the importance of acknowledging gifts of $100 and more with a phone call. That's right—all gifts of $100 or more. And if the gift, for any reason, seems to warrant a personal visit to hand-carry the receipt, consider this the best possible response.

Now, let me take you back to La Jolla, California. This time I can tell you the name of the organization. It's Scripps Institutions of Medicine and Science.

Scripps didn't need any prompting. For some time, they have been calling donors of $1000 and above, to thank them for their gift. During the conversation, they would tell donors how very important their gift was and how the gift would be used.

It was easy for them to move to calling $100 donors. Easy from the standpoint of accepting and adapting the concept. There was nothing easy, however, about making all of those telephone calls. In the case of Scripps, it amounted to over 5,000 calls a year.

I can hear you out there.

I know what you're saying. *It is absolutely impossible for me to spend that much time on the telephone making calls. I am too busy attending staff meetings, answering mail, going to committee meetings, and helping to put together the newsletter. And there are all of the special events, the dinners, the auctions, and the golf tournaments. And the meetings the boss calls that aren't planned or expected. And those days that the roof caves in first thing in the morning.*

Ahh, the tyranny of the unnecessary, the unexpected, and the unimportant!

I understand the time-constraints. The job is frantic, and increasingly turns up the speed on the treadmill of our lives. I do understand. But I must admit, that I have very little sympathy for the problem. After all, what is more important than thanking your donors! Think about it: What indeed is more important than thanking your donors?

Don't respond to the question yet. You can answer after you read on.

The extraordinary story I am about to relate begins about eight years ago when Scripps started calling its $100 donors. Dave Mitchell, the very bright and effective Vice President who headed the program at Scripps, understood the importance of these calls. He made a commitment that the calls would be made. There were all the reasons that every organization has for not doing them, but Dave was adamant and stubborn. He can be plenty adamant and down-right immovable when the situation calls for it. The $100 calls began. His determination is a trumpet that signals a call to all of us.

This is how this story begins. On an acquisition mailing, Scripps received a gift of $150 from a first-time donor. Here's what happened next. The donor received a call thanking him for the gift. The conversation from the donor on the other end was . . . well, judge for yourself.

"Have you folks made some kind of mistake? Are you certain you're calling the right person? I only sent a check for $150."

"You bet you're the one we want to talk with. This is the first time you have made a gift to Scripps and we want you to know how very important that donation is to us and how grateful we are. It really means a lot to us."

"Do you mean to tell me that you would take time to call for just a $150 gift? I can't believe it. Do you know that there are some gifts that I make that are much larger, and no one even bothers to send me a letter? Sometimes, I don't even get a receipt."

"Well, you need to know how very much your gift means to us. Let me take a minute and tell you how we're going to use your gift." And the staff person proceeds to talk about how the gift will be used.

"Well, I've got to tell you how impressed I am. It honestly never occurred to me that my gift would be that important to you. I am really pleased with the call. I'm impressed and delighted that it will be put to such good use."

Now it's three months later. Scripps receives another check from this donor. This time, it's for $10,000. And, again, he is called and thanked for his gift.

"You folks are really something. I can't believe that you're taking time to call again. I'm impressed and I want you to know how pleased I am that the gift is being put to such good use and that it means so much to you."

That's not the end of the story.

Later he sends another check for $10,000. And, of course—you guessed it—he is called on the telephone. This time, Dave Mitchell also makes a personal visit.

That's not the end of the story.

At the end of the year, he sends a check for $25,000.

Think of the giving, all of it from an acquisition mailing, supported and nurtured by appropriate appreciation. It started with $150, then $10,000, then another $10,000, then $25,000 more.

Then, one after another, came gifts of $500,000 . . . then $1.6 million . . . and another that followed for $2 million. Wow!

But wait. Yes, you guessed it. There's more. It just happened.

At a press announcement held in La Jolla, California, this donor revealed another gift. The donor gave a cash gift of . . . are you ready—of $100,000,000. Count the zeros! One hundred million dollars.

Now, it didn't just happen. There was a great deal of staff work that took place after the second gift. There are a lot of key people who contributed mightily to helping make that gift happen. But no one played a more significant role than Dave Mitchell. It was he who had the intuitive feeling, that second-sense, that there was something very special in this situation. Dave's antennae are always quivering!

After the third gift, Dave called on the donor. And after the year-end gift, Dave met with the donor's advisors. And then there was the careful deployment of staff to make certain that the donor received the proper attention and thanks. The appreciation was unending. There was never a gift that was more thoughtfully scripted, more scrupulously planned, more perfectly executed.

The first phone call didn't result in the final gift. But it unquestionably made it possible. You don't have to go to a costly seminar or attend a national conference to figure out that there's an important lesson here. It's so easy. Just do what your mother told you: *"Thank You" are the two most important words in the English language.*

There's one more gift I want to tell you about. It is a gift of spirit, awe, and magic. It's not as striking as the Scripps mega-donation, but it is every bit as dramatic. It is one of the most glorious major gifts I know about. A truly precious major gift.

I'll take you back to a very cold November day several years ago. A farmer walked into the office of Ginny Krueger. Ginny is the very thoughtful and sensitive Director of Development at North Valley Health Center in rural Warren, Minnesota. The farmer, bent with arthritis and in his 80s, was *scrubbed up* for town and wearing neatly pressed overalls and an obviously new flannel shirt. This was a special visit for him.

Ginny knew the farmer. She had spent time with him when his wife had died a few months earlier in the Health Center.

"About that fund drive you have, I'd like to do something for the hospital."

He laid an old checkbook on her desk. His hand was shaking. With great care, he slowly wrote $1000 in the proper blank and signed his name.

"You can fill in the rest. This is about all I have in the account, but it is something I really want to do because all of you were so wonderful to my wife, and to me."

Ginny was immensely touched. Who wouldn't be? If you looked closely, you could see the tears. Who could blame her?

A month later, Ginny baked some Christmas bread for her family. She decided she would take the farmer a loaf as a gift. There was something very special about him that she liked—and she knew his gift was an enormous sacrifice.

It was cold and getting dark when she started her drive—with the kind of heavy snow you expect in Minnesota in December. She kept driving out in the country until she finally found the old farmhouse where he lived. The house . . . well, it was worse than she anticipated. Tiny and sorely in need of repair. It suddenly occurred to her how truly sacrificial his gift was.

There was no doorbell. Ginny knocked on the door. The farmer finally answered. The door opened a crack. But when he saw her, he glowed. He invited Ginny into the living room. There was an old oil stove, a sagging couch, peeling wallpaper, and a few well-worn stuffed chairs with doilies to protect the arms. You get the picture.

Ginny gave him the Christmas bread. "Thanks again for your wonderful gift to the Health Center. It meant so very much to us."

He hugged Ginny. He asked her to wait a moment. The farmer came back with a pillowcase.

"My wife had been saving these bits and pieces for years. Every time there was a spare coin or dollar, she would put it in this pillowcase. She was saving it for something special. One night at the hospital, she told me that she knew she didn't have long to live. She told me to take the money in the pillowcase and to spend it on something that would really give me great joy and happiness. Maybe a trip—we had never left the farm. Or a new television set.

"I'd like to give the money to you, Ginny, for the hospital. You coming out here with the bread to thank me gave me more joy and happiness than words can ever say."

Five Important Guidelines To Ensure Your Success

1　**Say thanks**　The overriding, unforgiving principle that is so obvious in the stories is simple—say *thanks*. Donors expect it. More importantly, with the proper acknowledgment and appreciation, one gift will lead to another—and almost certainly, a larger one.

I make modest gifts to a dozen or so organizations where I live. There's a new Boys' and Girls' Club in town. It seems to me that every time I pass their building, there are a lot of kids around. At the end of last year, I sent them a check. It wasn't large, but large enough that it should have caught their attention. I waited until March, which seemed long enough, and then called to say that I had not received a receipt. I explained that I would like to have one and that legally, they were bound to send one. But legal or not, they should have sent an acknowledgment (I was being their fundraising consultant!). A month later, still no receipt. They will not be hearing from me at the end of next year.

I am not unlike most donors. I want to know that my gift, large or small, is greatly appreciated and that it will be put to important use. Donors want to know that what they have done, perhaps even in a small way, has made a significant difference in the life of a person.

2 **Make a time commitment** Make a determination now that you will deposit the check the day it is received. Insist that receipts and letters of acknowledgment are turned around in twenty-four hours. Okay, okay—forty-eight hours. But no more than that. I also like to suggest, by the way, that the office handwrite a simple *Thank You* on the face of the check. I know that individual donors go through their checks each month and it will not be lost on them that someone has taken the time to show appreciation.

I understand how impossible this is to do. I have heard that for years. I also know that when a commitment is made, when it is decided that this is something important and must be done—the program can be implemented. It starts at the top, with the chief. There has to be a determination at that level and there has to be the feeling on the part of the entire staff that this is something that really must be done. And it must.

The same with the receipts. If you decide that they are going to be sent out the next day, they will. If you think that there will be a problem in getting them out that fast, there will be. Yeats called it *the glow of achieving the impossible.*

Following the immediate turn-around of the receipt and acknowledgment, you can send out the special letters that are necessary—the one from the CEO for the large gift, and that sort of thing. And, of course, the telephone call. But first, and immediately, the acknowledging document and the receipt.

Am I talking about the possibility of two separate *thank-yous*? In some cases, you bet! More about that in a moment.

We did some market research once for a hospital and I remember a comment about the food: *The food is terrible, just horrible. And there isn't enough of it.* I was talking to Peter Levin who headed the hospital at Stanford University. It was an important lesson. He said: "You know, any hospital can have good food. There just has to be a determination from the administrator that the food here will be good. If the administrator makes the decision that this is important and is dogged about seeing that it will be done, the food will indeed be good. There's no reason or rationale for it to be otherwise."

3   **My rule of sevens**   Mary Roebling, a long time ago, taught me a very valuable lesson. She was the President of the Trenton (New Jersey) Trust Company. This was at a time when she was the only female CEO in the country of a major bank. I am not certain what she knew about a balance sheet, but she was one of the savviest marketing people I have ever worked with.

She told me once that if I could find a way to thank a person seven times for something, I would have them forever indebted to me. They would never forget how appreciative I was. I began applying *the principle of sevens* to fundraising. And you know, it works. It really does. I guarantee it.

When a person makes a gift to your organization, find a way to thank them seven times. Their gift will be larger the next year. I promise.

It's not as difficult as it sounds. Let's say, for instance, that a donor makes a gift to your camp program for a scholarship. But it could be to a college, hospital, or the Salvation Army. The principle is the same.

But let's use the camp as an example. The donor receives an acknowledging letter and a receipt immediately. The gift is large enough that it triggers a signal for the executive to send a letter or a personal note. If it's a handwritten note, all the better. *That's two thank-yous.*

A month later the Camp Director sends a letter, thanking the donor for the gift. *That's three.* During the season, a youngster, one of those who received the scholarship, sends a note, perhaps with a drawing. *That's four.*

At the end of the season, the Camp Director sends another letter. This can be a bit more formal, describing the end of the camp season and what a great year it was, the best in the camp's history. And then an explanation of how the donor helped make that possible. *That's five.*

Sometimes around Thanksgiving, the donor gets another note, a brief one, saying that, *Because of this special time of year, when we recount how thankful we are for our many blessings, I was reminded again of how particularly grateful I am for your gift and the scholarship you made possible. On behalf of all of the young people who benefited because of what you did* . . . or something of the sort. *That's six.*

And perhaps a card at Christmastime, or better still, at the beginning of the year with something such as, *You helped make this past year a glorious one for a lot of young people, because* . . . Wow! *That's seven.*

Work it out. Begin planning it now. Develop the design and the calendar. Begin thinking of how you can put those seven thank-yous into practice and place. Once you make the determination, it's really easy. You'll get the gift the following year. And it will be larger. I guarantee it.

4   **Old friends are the best**   There's always the sheer excitement, the high anticipation of an acquisition mailing. You sit at your desk, waiting for the returns.

You check them every day. *Will we get a good response to that spiffy package we developed? I must say, there's a heck of a lot of my own creativity in that mailing. Of course, if the returns are not quite as good as we thought . . .*

And, of course, in addition to the dollars—you hope to uncover some wonderful new friends. That's not unrealistic. Scripps did. Do keep in mind that old friends are indeed the best. Remember, your mother told you that, too. Your present donors deserve all of the nurturing, appreciation, and good stewardship you can shower on them. Drown them with attention.

My *Rule of Sevens*, by the way, will work wonders.

We know that it costs four to four-and-a-half times the energy, resources, and dollars to find a new donor as it does to keep one. Just remember the opening stanza of our old Fundraising Fight Song:

Acquisitions are mighty fine,
But renewals are more sublime.

(There is a great deal of fundamental truth in the rest of that anthem, and I would be pleased to hum it for you the next time we meet.)

Really work your present donor base. Show the kind of appreciation that is necessary. Let them know, on a regular basis, how important they are to the institution and those you serve. And develop a planned, specific, and written strategy for upgrading them.

5 **Regularly assess your effectiveness** On a regular basis, examine your status and progress.

A good test of how well you're doing is to take a look at the top fifty donors to your annual giving program.

Go ahead, try this. List the names of your top givers numerically—those who give the most listed first, and so on. Go back five years. By each name, list across the page the amount they have given in each of the past five years.

Here's what your grid will look like. You'll have fifty names running vertically down the left hand side. (There's no magic, by the way, to the number. If you have 35 or 40 top donors, that will be satisfactory, also.)

The next columns will show their giving five years ago, four years ago, and so forth.

Examine the list carefully. If all of your top donors have been giving for five straight years, you get high marks for nurturing, stewardship, and showing appreciation. It is obvious you are doing a good job of keeping them interested and committed.

You get low marks, however, because you haven't introduced any new sources to your donor base. You're in trouble. Your donors are getting older and you have not done anything to replace them.

Look at the list again. This time, run your finger horizontally across the page. If you see giving increasing consistently for the majority of your donors, you get high marks. You have done an excellent job of upgrading.

If you do not see any movement, it's a clear indication you have not worked at having your donors feel any sense of urgency about your service, your mission, or your vision. You have not made the case for new funds. Shame!

It's your job to keep that roster of key donors in a constant state of renewal and enhanced dedication to the institution. The list should grow, with new friends added on a regular basis. And there should be marked increases in giving by old friends.

It doesn't just happen. And it's never an accident. It requires a plan creatively conceived and a program implemented with determination.

It won't be easy. But remember, your mother also told you: *When the going gets tough, the tough get going.*

FASTRACK TENETS

The two most important words in the English language are: *Thank You.*

1   Say thanks. Never miss an opportunity. Let your donors know how important their gift is. And let them know how it is being used.

2   Make a commitment to send out receipts and acknowledgments in 24 hours, 48 hours at the most. When there is a determination to do this, it can be done.

    Special individual letters can be sent a little after that, along with the thanking telephone call. But first and immediately—the acknowledging document and the receipt.

3   Find a way to thank a person 7 times for their gift. Design a plan to do this and implement it. They will give the gift again—and they will give more. I guarantee it.

4   Your old friends are the best. Pursue renewals with all the vigor and ardor you can possibly muster. Consider any losses as a personal defeat. Design a planned, specific, and written strategy for upgrading them.

5   Carefully examine your effectiveness. Review the giving of your top 30 to 50 donors. Design a grid to determine the upgrading that has occurred over the past five years.

14

Breaking The Rules

I have spent a lifetime testing and challenging *the rules.* And breaking them!

I've followed Tom Peters' admonishment: "If it isn't broken . . . break it." I believe firmly that those who are most effective, the stand-outs in our field, stretch the boundaries, shatter the parameters, and seek new thresholds. They don't try to break out of the box. They create new boxes.

I can't help myself. I have a certain disinclination for time-honored ways and an irreverence for established procedures. I find no discomfort in that. Emerson said: ". . . a man must be a nonconformist, nothing is sacred but the integrity of your own mind."

As I confront and probe some of the hoary rules of our business, the grammar of our field, I've made some mistakes. But I've also found new mountain-tops. I am one with Steven Covey who admonishes us to *open the gate, the gate of change.*

There are some myths that persist, the nursery rhymes of our business. I'd like to address those I consider to be unfounded and most fallacious. Accept my explanation for now, but give thought and time to claim your own answers. Remember: fundraising is more an art than a science. In a letter to a young poet, Rainer Maria Rilke said: "Do not look for final answers now. They cannot be given to you because you have not yet lived them. It is a question of experiencing everything. For now, you must first live the question. Perhaps you will gradually, without ever noticing it, find yourself experiencing the answers, some distant day."

What I want you to do is your own examination, your own testing. Use that great philosopher Gertrude Stein as your beacon in bursting your own bubble-myths:

> There ain't no final answer.
> There ain't going to be any final answer.
> There has never been an answer.
> And that's the final answer.

(Be honest. Does anyone really understand Gertrude Stein?)

Myth #1: People give to meet the needs of an institution.

Wrong! Your organization does not have needs. Please follow my directions: Type out on a sheet of paper *Our Institution Does Not Have Needs. People Have*

Needs. Cut it out and tape it on your computer so that you see it every day.

Keep in mind: People have problems, they have concerns, and some live in agony. Your organization has the answer. You have the response. You have the solution to their needs.

For so long, I was doing it entirely wrong. I was selling what I considered to be *the need* of the organization. When I shifted from that to the need of those who were served, everything seemed to fall into place. I had been guilty of what George Eliot said of a professor in *Middlemarch:* "I was filled with the perfect liberty of misjudgment." And now I know better. I talk only about the needs of those who are served.

Try it. It works. Oh, I've been so guilty in the past. I have made captivating presentations talking about how great the need of the institution was. I wondered why my prospect yawned and their eyes glazed over. What really makes an impact is your immediate response and your solution to the needs of those you serve.

Myth #2: Staff is less effective in asking for gifts than volunteers.

I just read in a recent NSFRE piece that: *Successful fundraising officers do not ask for money. They get others to ask for it . . . the request to give should come from within the prospect's peer group.* That's simply not true. If you follow that dictum there will be a number of gifts you will miss.

All of the experience I have and the research I have done indicate clearly that donors give the most where they have high regard and a glowing esteem for a member of the staff, usually the CEO. The volunteer peer is quite often indispensable in opening the door and making the appointment. No matter how effectively coached, they are often not the best at asking for the gift.

For those major gifts that will help determine the success of a campaign or a program, I like sending the peer and the senior officer of the institution. I call this *The Magic Partnership*.

But at times you don't even need the volunteer. The other day, Raymond Cruitt returned from a visit with an alumnus. Raymond is the Associate Headmaster at the prestigious Asheville School. Ray called for the appointment himself. He had been calling on this person for several years. There was a close bonding.

Ray asked for $500,000 and got it. Would a volunteer have been better at making the ask? I seriously doubt it. Would Ray have done better by taking a volunteer with him? I think it would have been superfluous.

The important point is take who you need. But we do know in this business that: *getting the appointment is harder than getting the gift.* Use your volunteers to the utmost at opening the door and getting the appointment.

Myth #3: Professional fundraising consultants should never solicit for gifts.

The rationale is pretty much the same as above. I've done plenty of soliciting. And I love it. But I would never do it where I felt I was not the most effective person and the most appropriate.

I called on Samuel the other day in Naples, Florida. There were a lot of good reasons why we felt I was the person to make the contact. I could be direct with him in a way no one else could—and at the same time help him capture for himself the vision of the institution. I turned a $25,000 gift into $1 million. Oh certainly, someone else could likely have done it. The problem was, we couldn't think of anyone. I made the appointment myself and got the gift.

Who is the very most effective person in asking the chair of the board to make the sacrificial gift? It's not the staff, at least not in most cases. Not unless you are ready to circulate your résumé! And there isn't always a member of the board who can exert the kind of pressure necessary. As the *outside voice and architect* of the financial program, I'm the person in the best position possible to see how that gift can most mightily leverage the campaign.

I don't mind taking that role. As a matter of fact, I rather enjoy it. I find it an easy position to be able to say to the chair something such as: "I have nothing personally at stake in this program. It's really your project and everyone recognizes you as its leader. And almost certainly, my family and I will never be in a position to use your institution. But I can tell you this: If this campaign is to be successful and we are to gain the leadership and dollars we need, you play a role that no one else can. As the chair of this board, you really should make a gift of . . ."

Myth #4: Never take more than two people with you to make a call.

That simply isn't true. Take the marching band if that will help get the gift!

Personally, I prefer making a call by myself. It's my own hang-up but I feel that puts me in a bit more control. And I like that.

Best of all, I consider *The Magic Partnership* to be most effective. The chief executive officer and a volunteer who is a peer of the prospect is an irresistible combination.

The truth is, the more people you add, the more awkward it is. It isn't intimidating, it's just plain awkward. You end up having one or two who say nothing or very little at all. The prospect ends up thinking: *Who were those people and why did they come?* But if there's an understood and rehearsed role for each person, bring as many as you need.

Myth #5: Fundraisers need to work smarter, not longer.

I have never known of a time when there were greater demands on the fundraising staff. There seems to be no end. Wherever I go I ask the question, the same query I make at all of my seminars: Are you finding that you are working longer and longer, and seem to be getting less done? When I talk to senior staff around the country and query people at our seminars, I ask them what is the single dominating factor that keeps them from doing a more successful job. "I don't have enough time." That's what they tell me. Every one of them.

We used to tell the story about the new staff person who started off slowly in his job . . . and then tapered off. That's no longer possible. Today, you're expected to be running from the first day you start.

The problem isn't one of not working smart enough. There is simply more to be done and increasing demands. Most income fundraising budgets are up. And the drive to reduce expenses is unending. In most places there is less professional staff and fewer support staff, but a greater expectation to raise more and more funds.

We all want to work smarter, but it's tough. There are the committee meetings, the time with the boss, supporting our committee work, the extra stuff that needs to be done, the quarterly publications (that get out three times a year!), the phone that never stops ringing, the letters that must be read and answered, the twenty-seven e-mails (that are supposed to save us time).

Every day, it seems, the emergencies get in the way of what is really imperative. I find our professionals in the field are better and more effective than ever. I feel a deep sense of dedication and commitment on their part. And a devotion to do a really effective job. All of this is in better place than ever before. In many institutions, I believe the problem is that there is less support for the development effort.

Myth #6: Large gifts come from people of wealth.

They do indeed. But they also come, these large gifts, from those who are less obvious. There was the janitor at Bethany College in West Virginia, who somehow managed to put together an estate of over $1 million. He left it all to the College because: "Those students meant so much to me." And how about the cleaning woman at the Mississippi University who gave sufficient funds to establish two full scholarships? The list could go on.

At The Society For The Blind in Sydney, Australia, we called on a woman who made a gift of fifteen dollars. Why did we call on her? Why, for heaven's sake did we take the time to call on a fifteen dollar donor? I can't really explain. I saw the letter she wrote when she sent the check. I was greatly impressed with the depth of love she felt for this Society. It was compelling. I couldn't resist.

We took the receipt to her in person to thank her. One visit followed another. On the third visit, this woman of very modest means decided that she would leave her home, mortgage free, to the Society.

It's a wonderfully exhilarating business we are in. We do not know where our greatest surprises will come from. In Milwaukee, at the Red Cross, a farm worker left them $4 million in his estate.

The list goes on. Certainly, look for those high net worth people. That makes sense. But your mistake is grave if you don't look beyond to those with passion for the institution and have the capacity to do beyond what you can see above the surface. Probe. Examine. Look outside the box.

Myth #7: Ethnics don't give.

In a recent Gallup study, 87% of the ethnic universe that was queried said that they would give to charity—but were not asked.

In the next four years, thirty-four percent of our population will be African American, Asian, and Hispanic.

In San Francisco, we found that the *per capita* giving of the African American was higher than the rest of the population.

When Bill Crews, President of Golden Gate Seminary, took an Asian couple on a tour of the Seminary, he pointed to a spot on that beautiful campus where he hoped someday to build a library. "How much would a library like that cost," said the man, "that new library that you're talking about?"

Bill hadn't really given that a lot of thought. There were no architectural plans, no square footage, no figures. Just the dream and the vision. He said: "About seven million dollars."

The man turned to his wife and said: "I think we can do that, don't you?" "Yes," she replied. The gift was done. It was their first visit to the campus.

In one of the most prestigious independent schools in the country, the major gifts come from Asians. The United Way in Dade County (Miami) is flamed by the fervor of the Hispanic population. They get involved and they give.

It's quite clear. The ethnic population is here, and it is going to grow. In El Paso, the Latino population is now 88% and will grow to 92% in three years. Plenty of other cities are like that. *We have a responsibility to bring them into our circle.* They need to take prominent positions on boards, they need to become involved, and they need to be asked. That's the point—they need to be involved and asked. And that's our responsibility.

Myth #8: Baby Boomers don't give.

The evidence indicates otherwise. This past year, the Boomers turned 50. We know that in the next six years, $11.4 trillion will be passed from one generation to the next. (That's trillion!) Some think it will be even more than that. The Boomers will be the recipient of this largesse. It's a significant concern to us to know if there is a philanthropic-bent.

Everywhere I go, I ask the question: "Do you think the Baby Boomers give as much as their parents?" Virtually all agree they don't. But dig a little.

What we know now, and the evidence is clear, is that where they are involved in programs, where they serve on the board, where they are brought into what I call *the institutional hug*—they give, and they give generously.

But they're a special breed, these Boomers. They are deeply touched by those things that affect them and in which they are involved. *Involvement* is the word. If you don't involve them, get them to participate, ask them to serve, don't get them into your *institutional hug*—you will not get their gift.

But that's the same for their mom and dad—the more they're involved, the more they love you, and the more they love you the more they give. It's as simple as that.

When I speak at our seminars, as often as possible I try to interview a philanthropist. We both sit on bar stools (kitchen stools for you Baptists!) and we have a spontaneous session. There are no planned questions, nothing very rigid. Half of the folks I interview are Boomers. They have become involved and have learned the joy of giving. They are passionate about their institutions. They are challenging, probing, looking for a great cause.

The other half I interview are the older generation. When I ask the question about whether they feel their children are as engaged and as generous as they are, their reply is almost always something such as: "As best as we can remember, they are about where we were at that age." They are convinced that the younger group will be as generous when their time comes. "Don't worry about them," Martha Ingram (extraordinary Nashville philanthropist and volunteer) says. "When the time comes, they'll be there and do even more than we have."

Get them involved, these Boomers. That's your ticket. Move them into positions of leadership. That's the road to success. Get them to give. That first gift will be difficult, just like the first time you tried to ride a bike. After that, the rest is easy.

Myth #9: You can go to the well too often.

I hear this all the time—mostly from uninitiated volunteers. No offense meant!

We know from all the studies and all the work we do that the more people give, the more they give. Giving begets giving. Your largest gifts will come from those who have already given.

In a campaign, for instance, when you are very close to goal, but can't seem to raise the little bit extra that you need to claim success—what do you do? You go to all of those who have not yet given or to those who said: "See me a little bit later and I'll make a gift." You go to these sources to put you over goal. Wrong! You go to those who have already made major contributions, your most generous donors. You ask them for a second gift. They're the ones who will put you over.

I was talking with McClain Bybee the other day. He's the brilliant chief behind the powerful fundraising that is done at Brigham Young University. McClain was telling me about the horrible mistake that had been made recently with one of their direct mail pieces. They meant to send a mailing to all alumni who had not yet given. Somehow, the Mail House got it messed up and instead of the mailing going to the delinquent, it went to those who had already given. "We were in a panic," McClain reports. "I was so concerned that our alumni who had just given from a previous mailing would be terribly upset to receive another request. I was amazed with what happened. We got a 40% response from the second mailing." We shouldn't be surprised. Those who give, give more.

Those who make Planned Gifts tend to make larger and larger annual gifts. And if asked, they will do another Planned Gift. And make provisions for an Estate gift.

Here's my rule. Live by it. I do. "You will be hurt more by those who would have said *yes*, but were not asked—than by those who say *no*."

Myth #10: Tax is a prime motivator in getting the gift.

I wish it were. If tax really did clinch the gift, we estimate in this country there would be 5.5 times the giving that there now is.

Think of it, 5.5 times. Do some math. It boggles the mind. At 5.5 times the current giving, if tax were truly the prime incentive, we would have $825 billion given to philanthropy. What a glorious array of services that would provide to meet the human and social agendas of this country. Tax alone is not the answer.

George Weyerhauser told me: "Oh, it certainly isn't tax. Some years I give too much. Some years I don't give enough. I never really think about it." Marianne McDonald says: "Tax? Of course not! Hey, I'm trying to save the world. I'm trying to make a real difference. When you're trying to save the world, you don't think about tax."

Certainly, everyone takes into account any advantage there might be. They would be silly not to. And sure, it does in some situations help determine the timing. All of that is true. My careful examination and probing of forty men and women who committed to $1 million gifts and over told me that tax is one of the lowest on the scale of motivating factors. That was consistent throughout the analysis.*

George Gallup found the same thing when he did his study, a cross-section of the nation. People give to change lives and save lives. Folks were clear that tax was not a prime factor. In fact, most indicated that they did not understand the tax implications at all.

No, don't sell the tax. Instead, be passionate about the vision and mission of your institution. That's what will sell. Tax alone won't do it. I promise you. Your donors are guided, as Milton wrote: by faith and matchless passion.

Myth #11: The factors that make a great salesperson are the same that make a great fundraiser.

Well, I think that's mostly true but not entirely. Many attributes are common to both. Perseverance, certainly. A sense of humor—although not many would

---

* *Mega Gifts*, Precept Press, 1983.

think of putting that on the list this, is indeed important. A self-starter. High expectations. A commanding presence. A willingness to work long hours. High energy. A high tolerance for ambiguity. The list goes on.

But there are a number of essential factors that are common within the really great fundraisers. Integrity leads the list. You would hope for that in a salesperson but it wouldn't be essential. In a fundraiser, it leads the list. Without it, nothing else is important.

Integrity is important because it is the enabling quality that girds the fundraiser's profile. Integrity and ethics aren't a sometimes thing. In fundraising, they are everything.

Potter Stewart, the highly esteemed former Supreme Court Justice, knew something about ethics and integrity. He said: "Ethics is understanding the difference between knowing what you have the right to do . . . and knowing what is the right thing to do." Justice Stewart said that he was talking about being unafraid to give your pet parrot to the town gossip.

The effective fundraiser brings a passion to the work. For the really good ones, it is a love affair. "Filled with flame, passion, and spirit," is the way Dr. Samuel Johnson put it. Ahh, that really describes the great ones in our field. Montaigne said: "My work is my life." The great ones really believe that.

You should have the same passion for your work as you do for your hobby. If you don't feel that passion, commitment, and joy—chances are you're in the wrong profession. Get out of fundraising.

And an important distinction I draw is that the salespersons sell their product. The really effective fundraisers *listen the gift.* As you know by now, listening is one of the most significant factors in securing the gift.

The most capable in our profession understand that those asking the questions are in control of the conversation. Attorneys examining and probing a witness is a prime example. By their very questions, they direct the content of what the judge and jury hears. An effective fundraiser should spend no more than a quarter of the time in talking and the balance, in listening.

Myth #12: There are campaigns that are successful that don't have powerful Boards.

That's true, but the odds are strongly against you. All of the evidence clearly demonstrates that the board leads the way. It determines the future of the organization.

Of all the responsibilities of the board, I consider the very most important that—of not allowing a deficit. And I don't refer to a financial deficit. I mean a *Mission Deficit.*

Any board can balance the budget. You simply cut out services and programs, you release staff, pay inadequate salaries, and perform low or medium standard work instead of high quality. You simply bring down the expenses to meet the income.

An effective board provides sufficient income to meet whatever expenses are necessary to serve the mission and vision of the institution. Sister Monica at Sacred Heart Medical Center in Eugene, Oregon, said to her board: "No margin, no mission." That says it all.

To generate major funds, you need men and women who can bring influence and affluence to their positions. You want board members with passion. Roaring advocates. Dedicated and devoted board members are beyond calculation and are always at the very heart of any significant achievement and cause.

The more a person is involved in an institution, the greater the inclination to a gift. Here's something that emphatically proves the point. At one of the premier independent schools in the country, a study was made of board giving. They looked at the average giving before the person became a board member and after. Before—$1,694 a year. After—$24,120 a year. This is one example. We see it in every single study we do. I'm certain it doesn't surprise you. The board leads the way. In order to raise significant funds, you need a significant board.

Myth #13: Prospects need a great deal of cultivation before making a large gift.

I know, I'm just certain that I'm going to be called a traitor on this one. For years, I've been singing the hymn of nurturing fundraising.

I'm a roaring proponent of *Moves Management*. In my version, I call it **T•A•G** (Time•Action•Goals)—but call it what you want, just so you have in place a process for ensuring the optimum cultivation of your prospects and the ongoing stewardship of your donors. I preach that sermon at every seminar I conduct and in all my speeches. I make certain that all of our clients have a working and effective system in place.

I'm an apostle of Si Seymour. He said that a major giver is like a pickle. Well, I'm paraphrasing a bit. But he said you don't make a pickle out of a cucumber by sprinkling a little vinegar over it. You've got to immerse it in vinegar.

I don't want anyone to give up their *Moves Management* program. I think it's terribly important, essential to an effective-running development office. So don't start writing letters to my publisher.

There are two factors, however, I want you to consider. The first is that a number of your donors are ready, ready right now, to make a major gift. There's no consequential value to making a dozen more contacts. Your donors are ready!

The second factor is that a request for a gift is actually a very positive step in the cultivation process. Every major gift that is made is a launching pad for the next one. Only the next one will be larger.

Go for it! I want you to begin practicing, at least on a limited basis, the concept: Ready. Fire. Aim. You know what? You will be successful in more cases than not. TNT—that's what I preach: Today Not Tomorrow!

I confess to you something that has caused me great concern. With one of our clients, one of the largest fundraising machines in the country, most gifts derived are from direct mail and special events. I started them off on a program of *Moves Management*. The process and mechanics were all in place. It was a thing of beauty. Everyone bought into the concept and they were on their way.

It would remind you of elephants mating. It was a marvel to behold. It made a lot of noise. And it made the ground shake.

The problem is that after nearly twelve months of cultivation and calls, not one prospect has yet been asked for a gift. It is a pure case of Ready, Aim, Aim, Aim . . .

The prospects for these major gifts are all donors, people who love the organization. Their gifts to date have not been of major consequence but many have been giving for years and years. They simply have not been asked to increase their giving.

I admit to doing a disservice to our client. Consultants don't often fess up to this sort of thing! It was entirely appropriate for me to take them into a *Moves Management* program. But at the same time, I should have put into place an active, one-on-one, soliciting program. Remember, you miss 100% of the shots you don't take.

So don't give up your nurturing and cultivation. Just begin an aggressive program of asking for the gift.

I want you to start asking. Now. Be unafraid of making mistakes, knowing that the only road to success is the struggle. You'll win more than you lose. If you don't get the gift this time, you'll get it the next. I want you to **Fall Forward Fast**. **FFF**—that's it. Make the call, make the ask. To be turned-down is never fatal or final. To not make the attempt is the great failure.

Myth #14: Women are different than men in their giving.

That's what I thought until I found out differently. So I don't blame you at all for being on the wrong track! You may consider yourself unrebuked.

Let me tell you how my search began. Three or four years ago, there was a great deal of material and a number of articles about how different women are than men in their giving. We were bombarded with information. There was study after study. We were drowning in data.

I kept thinking: this is really hard to believe, but these folks must be onto something. So I came up with the idea for a new book. My publisher was excited about the prospect, too. I had visions of royalties dancing in my head. I even had a working title: *Women Who Give.*

I conducted a great deal of market research. In addition, I interviewed sixteen women, each of whom had made at least one gift of $1 million—and most made a number of gifts of that size.

After the sixteen interviews, I stopped the research. I called off the book.

What I found is that there are no factors that you can categorize as being women-driven or male-oriented. I had no book. I agreed with Eleanor Roosevelt who said that the only possible disadvantage women have is in climbing trees.

It was a wonderful lesson and reminder for me. Every one of your donors is a glorious human being, a person of great hopes and dreams. And disappointments and problems. High aspirations and expectations. And periods of deep valleys and doldrums.

Note this well. Each one of your prospects and donors, male or female, is a unique individual—*rara avis*, a rare bird. No two are really alike. Once you understand that, you'll be able to relate to these wonderful people on an individual basis, man or woman.

At my seminars, I almost always ask the group if they feel there are different factors that motivate the giving of men and women. Most of the heads nod in the affirmative. I ask in what way. "Well women are much more emotional in their giving." "Women really like to get involved in the program." "Women like a lot more information and detail."

Or, "Women are willing to get involved in the more venturesome projects, and men stay with the conventional." Those that say that haven't met Dede Williams, who chaired the Museum and the Grace Cathedral campaigns in San Francisco. That's pretty conventional stuff.

The business about women wanting more detail and information than men, that's simply a generalization without merit or base. No one who has worked with an engineer would dare say such a thing.

Or women are more emotional in their giving, that's another old wives (old husband's?) tale. W. Clement Stone, the great Chicago philanthropist, told me that when he gets ready to write a check for a gift, he is so excited and emotionally involved, he can barely hold the pen to write the check.

Throw away all of those articles and preconceived ideas about how different women are in their giving. Go ahead, throw them away!

Get to know your donor with, as Milton wrote, "heart-filled examination and matchless fortitude." Get inside their heart and their head. You will find a spirit, incomparable and transcendant, ready to take flight. Approach them, both men and women, as uncommon individuals. It will be the wind beneath their wings.

I heartily endorse the major emphasis we now give to involve women in our leadership and fundraising programs. Of course. It was overdue. They live longer than we do. They divorce better. Well, don't take offense, they do. And more and more, in many families, they are driving the gift. And of significance, of those in the country with a Net Worth of $500,000 or more, 47% (and growing) are women.

Myth #15: People give to people.

This is perhaps the oldest of our venerable fundraising verities and . . . probably the most misunderstood and least factual. I know there will be some who will want a place reserved for me *below* for such blasphemy. But it simply isn't true.

People give to great causes, and to meet urgent and compelling needs. They give to institutions in whose vision and dreams they can identify. They give to programs that seize the soul and spirit.

Peel back the layers of misguided "truths" until you get to the very core of what truly motivates. If you don't, you may not get the gift you deserve.

For starters, if *people give to people*—it's most likely because of the high regard for one of the staff, usually the chief executive officer. But it could also be a physician who calls on a grateful patient. Or a camp director who calls on a former camper. Or a faculty member, beloved by one of his students. That sort of thing does indeed make the statement come alive.

But to think that a person will make a large gift simply because a peer or a friend (a friend is very often the worst person to make a call and the least likely from whom to get a good gift) is involved, could put you on the road to disappointment.

I ask this question all the time. The response is consistently the same. I was with Chris Hellman the other day. She is that extraordinary Chair of the San Francisco Ballet who, with her husband, raised more money than any other ballet company in the country. In a completely unrehearsed session, I was asking her questions at one of our seminars.

I asked her what happens when you call on others for a gift, let's say for the Ballet—do you think that it's quite likely that they will call on you for one of their beloved causes? "Of course. I know they will. It happens all the time. If you call on a dozen people for major gifts for the Ballet, you can count on twelve visits and requests from them."

"Do you always give to them?" I asked. "Do you feel some sense of obligation?"

"No I don't. It's extremely difficult because some of these people are friends and because some made very large gifts to my pet project. But if Warren and I don't really feel keenly about the cause, we don't make the gift. We explain why and hope they understand. Most often they do, but sometimes it strains the relationship. So be it."

Stanley Marcus (Dallas' Mr. Neiman-Marcus) told me that he loves calling on people for projects that are important to him. "I want people to know how keenly I feel about certain programs. But I certainly would not make a large gift to something I didn't care greatly about, no matter who called on me. I don't think that happens."

People give to exciting and bold ventures. They give to change lives and save lives. That's why they give. And it is often without regard as to who makes the call.

But here's the compelling lesson. There are those important men and women, peers, who can make appointments for you and open doors. That's the key. We know in this business that it's *harder to get the appointment than it is to get the gift*. All of my research bares this out. Use those key people to make the appointment. But don't expect the large gift unless you are able to get your arms around the prospect and bring him or her into your *institutional hug*.

I think of Lord Chesterfield who said about Macaulay: "I wish I knew as much about anything as Maculay claims to know about everything." For some, new ways can be threatening. There are those wedded to the old, and they may be highly intolerant of bursting these fundraising bubbles. Robert Lowell said: "All great truths begin as blasphemies."

There are those who are prisoners of their procedures. Test these ideas for yourself. It may not be easy. John Maynard Keynes said: "The greatest problem is not to get people to accept new ideas, but to make them forget about the old ones." I'm with Keynes. I want you to join me in breaking some of these old, creaky rules— myths of the past. Break some of your own. Don't be limited to my fifteen myths.

I've done my best, had my say, sung my song. Writing is really tough. But what is immensely difficult is to know when to stop!

FasTrack tenets

This chapter covered fifteen myths that are most prevalent in our work. Turn those into positive statements and you have the most basic elements to build a foundation for a winning and successful fundraising program.

1   Don't talk and write about the needs of your institution. Instead, talk about how you are uniquely positioned to serve the needs of people.

2   For some prospects, staff can be extremely effective in asking for gifts—more so than volunteers. But pair together staff and volunteer—and you have a magic partnership.

3   There are certain situations and certain prospects when your professional fundraising consultant is in an excellent position to talk to one of your prospects about a gift. Don't dismiss this possibility out of hand.

4   There's no magic to the number of people who should go on a call for a gift. Take as many people as you need—no more, no less.

5   My observation is that fundraisers are more effective than ever before. They are certainly better trained, and they work harder and longer hours. If there is any deficiency, it is that there is more to be done and it has to be achieved with fewer support staff.

6 Look beyond those with high Net Worth for your larger gifts. You will find that there isn't a direct relationship between large gifts and high Net Worth. There are those who will delight and surprise you who have been overlooked.

7 African Americans, Asians, and Hispanics will give. There is ample evidence of this. You simply need to get them actively involved. Get them into your *institutional hug.*

8 Baby boomers will give to your organization. There are unshakeable data that they are more generous than their parents were at the same age. They are passionate about those programs in which they become involved, but they are interested in outcomes and results. You won't win their loyalty unless you can demonstrate prime service and good work.

9 The more people give, the more they give. Good giving begets even better giving. You will receive your largest gifts from those who already give.

10 A tax incentive is not the prime reason that a person will make a major gift to your organization. What really counts is a belief in the mission of the institution. Hammer away at your mission. That's what will win the gift.

11 Being effective in sales has nothing to do with being a truly successful fundraiser. What is required in our field is impeccable integrity, a skill in listening, and passion for the institution.

12 Your campaign will do significantly better if you have a strong board—trustees who can make and influence large gifts. If you don't have that kind of a board, you can still win a campaign but it's some-

what like going to battle without the proper ammunition.

13   Proper cultivation and nurturing are significant factors in securing a major gift—but keep in mind that some of your prospects are ready now to make their contribution. Added cultivation will only delay the ask. Review carefully whether you should ask for the gift now. And keep in mind that every time you ask for a gift is actually an important cultivation step that leads you one step closer to an even larger gift.

14   It is impossible to differentiate and segment the factors that motivate a woman to give. Some feel that the rationale is different than what motivates a man. Not true! Each of your prospects is a wonderfully unique person with his or her own distinct set of characteristics, passions and interests. Find out in each case, man or woman, what will motivate him or her.

15   People give to causes out of a deep commitment to the mission of the organization. They give to relevant, emotionally appealing, and urgent programs. Having the *right person* ask for the gift will help carry the day, and this is often a staff person. Leverage will count a great deal in opening the door and getting the visit.

Some of the material in this book first appeared in columns I wrote for *Contributions*, one of the most highly regarded publications in the field of fundraising. I felt that some of the columns were quite suitable to include. Their voice harmonises well with the message I wanted to deliver. If you thought you had seen some of the fabric from this bolt of cloth before, this probably explains it. But I don't mind the repetition. That's what good sermons are all about. Someone asked the great poet and philosopher George Santayana if, in his old age, there were many things he would like to change in his writing. He said there weren't. *"I feel I have much the same things to say—but I wish to say them in a different tone of voice."*

—J. P.

Appendix

The Fundraiser's Guide to Listening©

RATING SCALE		TOTAL POINTS	YOUR LISTENING QUOTIENT
Frequency	Points		
Always	5	261 to 285	Outstanding—you're great!
Almost Always	4	216 to 260	You're a good listener, but work on those areas that still require attention.
Usually	3	171 to 215	You're a fair listener, but you should work on your weaknesses.
Sometimes	2		
Seldom	1	Below 171	Active listening is an acquired talent—you should make an effort to improve your skills.
Never	-2		

CONCENTRATION	POINTS
1 When I talk with others, my mind is completely absorbed by what they are saying and it doesn't wander.	
2 In a conversation, I hold my comments until the other person is finished talking, even though my comments may have direct relevance to what he or she is saying.	
3 I do not let interruptions, like ringing telephones or people walking by, distract my attention from what the person is saying.	

4 I consistently keep eye contact with the person I'm talking with.	
5 I make certain I avoid the *mind-reading syndrome*. That's where I determine what I believe the person is thinking without listening carefully to what the person is actually feeling and saying.	
6 When I talk with someone, I have a better recollection of what they said as opposed to what I said.	
7 I listen without judging or being critical.	
8 I concentrate on the person's meaning and message rather than how he or she looks.	
9 I make certain not to daydream while someone else is talking.	
10 I concentrate completely on what is being said, even if I am not totally interested.	
11 I can truly say that in most of my conversations, I feel a sincere interest and an inquiring curiosity.	
12 I listen to the other person's view, even if it differs from mine.	
13 I don't stop listening even if I'm fairly certain I know what the other person is going to say.	

The Fundraiser's Guide to Listening

ACKNOWLEDGING	
14 I build on previous responses by asking follow-up questions to statements just made.	
15 I make certain that the other person knows I am listening by giving brief, encouraging acknowledgments—such as: *I see, really, that's interesting,* and so forth.	
16 I make it a practice not to interrupt.	
17 In a discussion, clearly more than half of my time is spent in listening rather than talking.	
18 When appropriate, I reinforce and affirm the other's view by restating their position.	
19 I am able to empathize with the person I'm having a discussion with—I can truly tell *where they are coming from.*	
20 I regularly repeat or paraphrase to make certain I understand what the person is feeling and saying.	
21 I really work and think about motivating the other person to talk by demonstrating a physical and mental attentiveness and showing expressions of interest.	

The Fundraiser's Guide to Listening

22 I am careful about not sending the wrong non-verbal messages—moving to a closed-body position, impatiently tapping fingers on a desk, and so forth.	
23 I make certain that when the other person is talking and looks at me, what they see is a happy reflective, responsive appearance.	
24 I demonstrate my understanding and caring with my body language—leaning forward, nodding my head in approval, arching my neck, my facial appearance, and so forth. I give every evidence of riveted attention.	

STRUCTURING

25 Prior to a meeting, I establish my objectives and prepare myself to listen.	
26 When I talk with others, I make mental notes of major ideas, key points, and supporting reasons.	
27 I listen for priorities, sequence, and emphasis.	
28 I move from the general to the specific when I am trying to order or organize the speaker's viewpoint or argument.	
29 I ask for clarification or elaboration regarding the speaker's viewpoint—	

to ensure proper interpretation and complete understanding of the rationale.	
30 I attend to all promised actions, however great or small, following a discussion.	
RELATIONSHIP BUILDING	
31 When I talk with someone, I encourage a two-way flow of communication by asking open-ended questions.	
32 I let others know that I am trying to understand what they are saying by using phrases such as *Tell me more about that* or *Can you give me an example?*	
33 I encourage people to express their true feelings about an issue.	
34 I ask people what they expect from a given action or relationship.	
35 I seek information that will allow me to understand the speaker's framework and context so that I can properly interpret what I am hearing.	
36 I prepare for my meeting in advance by reading, reviewing, and finding out as much as possible about the person I'll be talking with.	

The Fundraiser's Guide to Listening

37 In a conversation, I clarify, probe, and question.	
38 I attempt to gather more information about the other person by asking questions.	
39 I work at learning something from each person.	
40 I practice regularly to increase my listening efficiency.	
SENSITIVITY	
41 When I am talking with others I read their body language as well as listen to their words, in order to fully interpret what they are telling me.	
42 In effective listening, the non-verbal communication the person sends me is as important as the verbal, and I am alert to that—facial expressions, posture, eye contact, tapping fingers, checking the time, a poker face, tight facial muscles, frowning, and so forth.	
43 I listen to what the speaker is saying, both verbally and non-verbally.	
44 I try not to memorize a conversation but rather absorb the feeling and intent of the message.	

The Fundraiser's Guide to Listening

45 I listen to more than the words themselves—I hear the emotional tone of the person, the pitch, the subtle variations that might indicate displeasure, and so forth.	
46 I try to read what's going on behind their spoken words by asking myself what they might be feeling, why they are saying it, and what is implied by what they say.	
47 In a listening mode, I am particularly sensitive to how a person, familiar or not, may feel about being touched—knowing that some people do not like it.	
PERSONAL CONCERNS	
48 Before a conversation with a key person, I make certain my energy level is as high as possible because I know fatigue is a barrier to good listening.	
49 I'm careful about personal habits that may be distracting to the person I'm talking with—chewing gum, biting nails, etc.	
50 I make certain, as much as possible, that the physical environment is appropriate for effective conversation—the music is not too loud, the temperature is correct, and so forth.	

The Fundraiser's Guide to Listening

51 I dress in a way and make certain my appearance is such that I do not detract from the conversation.	
52 I care greatly about people and those I meet and talk with can sense that in my listening.	
53 I try to assume a *leveling posture* where my eyes are on a straight line with the person I'm talking with.	
54 I'm careful to avoid anything that provides a negative connotation: raising an eyebrow, looking away, rolling my eyes, behaving restlessly, slumping, drumming my fingers, swishing my foot, and so forth.	
55 I go into an important session knowing the kinds of questions I'm going to ask and the manner in which I will ask them.	
56 If the person has negative feelings about me or the Institution, I do not become defensive.	
57 I attempt to arrange the seating so that the prospect is comfortable and in a manner conducive to direct eye contact and communication.	
58 I love my work and I enjoy life—and I believe this helps make me a better listener.	
TOTAL:	

PROSPECT EVALUATION GRID

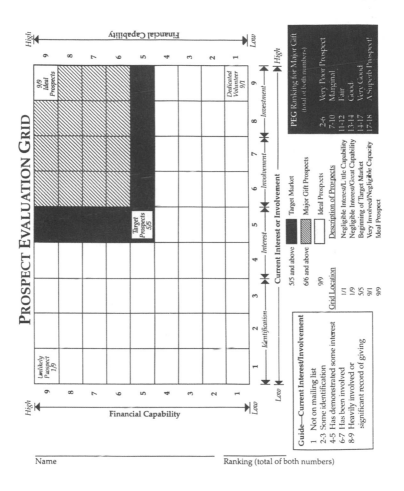

Name _____

Ranking (total of both numbers) _____

Prospect Evaluation Grid